"Sometimes I can't help but parables, thinking to myself, 'What was that all about?' Which is why what Samuel Hughes is up to in *Jesus Stories* is so very important! Through a blend of Bible exploration and real-life experience, Samuel is personalizing the parables for us, helping us apply their timeless truths in the here and now."
—*Trent Sheppard, author of* Jesus Journey

"I was deeply blessed by Samuel's wisdom and insights into Jesus' parables. As Samuel unfolded the deep, affective meaning of the parables, I was drawn into Jesus' loving intention for us and challenged to seek after him more whole-heartedly. The fresh unfolding of the heart of *Jesus Stories* makes it a very worthy read."
—*Dr. Bruce A. Demarest, Professor of Theology and Spiritual Formation, Denver Seminary, author of* Satisfy Your Soul, Seasons of the Soul, *and* Soul Guide

"What do you do when you cannot pray? We've all had those moments. Before we even sit down, we sense the dread of a routine that's empty. It didn't used to be this dry. Our prayer time was rich; our Bible reading came alive; but recently, all that has disappeared. So, what do we do? For one, we need to have a variety of tools in our spiritual toolbox. That's what Samuel's treatment of the parables can become for us—a rich, focused source of new inspiration. Not only does Samuel provide a clear and concise understanding of each parable he treats, he also walks us imaginatively into each scene; opening the door as it were into the house where a lost coin is frantically searched for on the floor, or letting us get our fingers in the dirt as we uncover in a field a treasure beyond our wildest imagination, or sitting in the midst of the laughing music of the father's prodigal party as we watch the dancing and hugging. What Samuel does is train us to do this imaginative Scripture reading for ourselves. And that's the best sort of spiritual guide we can hope for, a coach who leads us in the drills of grace and trust, so that when we do get into the game our skills have become part of us."
—*Robert Moore-Jumonville, Ph.D., Professor of Christian Spirituality, Spring Arbor University, author of* Jogging with G.K. Chesterton, *and* The Hermeneutics of Historical Distance

"'Tell me a story,' these words echo through all our meaningful relationships. With a blend of contextual background, modeling the practice of imaginative prayer, and inviting the reader into an experience with the storytelling of Jesus, Hughes delivers an opportunity to encounter the love of our Savior. Learning to listen to these stories with mind and heart attuned to application, the reader will experience a book designed to taste and see that the Lord is good. Herein is an adventure through imaginative prayer into right living. This book serves as a doorway into the house where Jesus is the host; you would do well to spend the night."

—*Daniel T. Haase, Associate Lecturer of Christian Formation & Ministry, Wheaton College*

"Samuel's storytelling invites me in and makes me feel like I am visiting with Jesus one-on-one. In his casual but detailed portrayals of the greatest Storyteller of all, Samuel brings new life to Jesus' timeless and tender care for us. *Jesus Stories* offers interactive ways to bring more of God's love into our own everyday experience."

—*Theresa Wyatt Prebilsky, author of* Rosetears

"Not since Dr. Craig Blomberg's *Interpreting the Parables*, have I been so captivated by a book on the parables of Jesus. What makes *Jesus Stories* unique is that Samuel Hughes creatively looks at each parable in the book of Luke through the eyes of someone in the crowd who heard Jesus tell the story. What an amazingly fresh look at the parables! I commend *Jesus Stories* to you. I promise you will see the parables with new eyes."

—*Dr. Larry Lindquist, Senior Professor of Leadership, Denver Seminary*

Jesus Stories

Awakening to Love through His Parables

Samuel C. Hughes

RIVER BIRCH PRESS

Daphne, Alabama

ISBN 978-1-951561-93-2 (print)
ISBN 978-1-951561-94-9 (e-book)
For Worldwide Distribution
Printed in the U.S.A.

River Birch Press
P.O. Box 868, Daphne, AL 36526

Contents

Acknowledgments

What a joy to be at this point in my writing journey. I owe special thanks to the folks at River Birch Press for believing in this book. I have to say thank you to Keith Carroll for providing good suggestions and for carrying the torch of helping endorse this project.

I owe a special gratitude to Pat Wight, for masterfully guiding me through the Ignatian Exercises years ago. The experience was life changing, and it gave me a deep love for imaginative prayer. Few people live out the love of God like this wonderful lady.

Thanks to some special people who took the time to look over *Jesus Stories* and provide written endorsements; Trent Sheppard, the late Bruce Demarest (we lost a good one), Larry Lindquist, Robert Moore-Jumonville, Dan Haase, and Theresa Prebilsky. A special shout out to my friend Jeff Daley for providing much-needed early suggestions and encouragement.

But easily, I am most indebted to my dream girl, my beloved wife of 41 years (you read that right!), Tina. She was my rock when I needed someone to lean on. She was my sounding board when I talked way too much about this project. And she was my editor-in-chief on so many occasions.

I am thankful for my entire family, my two incredible sons, Micah and Mark, and their amazing wives, Avrey and Erin. My boys sure know how to pick 'em. And I'm sure glad the gals said yes. And a final shout-out to my three special granddaughters; Ella, Zion, and Hannah. I hope you fall in love with the Storyteller and cherish His tales. I know you will. Jesus sure loves you, and so do I.

Preface

We all love a good story. As children, it was often the last thing we heard as we drifted off to sleep. As adults, we still enjoy them, not so much to put us to sleep but to wake us up! A good story has the unique power to motivate us, challenge our behavior, and even change our core beliefs. A story, unlike facts alone, can grab our hearts and touch our emotions.

We crave stories, whether read, watched, or listened to. Yet most people ignore the best Storyteller ever, Jesus! That's right, Jesus was a master at it. His stories, called parables, are remarkably practical—sometimes funny, often peculiar, and always packing a heartwarming yet rather uncomfortable punch. Jesus was sometimes flat-out ornery with His stories, but one thing is for sure, if we experience them, we are bound to fall in love with the Storyteller. Why? His stories are designed with you in mind. And they contain nuggets of wisdom to live by.

Jesus' stories aren't meant to be strictly analyzed as one might obsess over the fine details of a sports car, fixating on the owner's manual and keeping the car spotlessly clean while it sits unused in the garage. No, Jesus' stories are to be experienced. We are to hop in and take them for a spin; put the top down and feel the rush of emotions.

Jesus knew a story was a powerful platform for teaching truth. And the power lies within our imagination. You see, stories are most effective if we join in with our hearts more than our heads. Using one's imagination with Scripture is by no means a new form of experiencing God. Saint Ignatius, founder of the Jesuits, pioneered it some 500 years ago.

The great gift that Saint Ignatius gave the world was imaginative prayer—praying with Scripture by putting oneself in the story. Instead of simply reading about Jesus, Ignatius encouraged entering in and experiencing Jesus. By doing so, we watch Jesus—His gestures, the look in His eyes, and the expression on His face. We hear Him speak the words of Scripture. Better yet, we hear Him speak specifically to us in warm and loving ways.

Imaginative prayer allows Jesus to penetrate our heart that intellect alone cannot touch. Imaginative prayer engages our feelings, and it transforms the Jesus of the Gospels into our Jesus—a Friend we know, admire, and interact with.

How do we know we are to engage with the parables in this way? The simple reason is that Jesus asked us to do so. Jesus often started His parables with an invitation. Jesus says, "Suppose you have a friend, and you go to him at night with a need." Or "If you'd want to build a tower, wouldn't you first sit down and consider its cost?" Or "Suppose you had a hundred sheep, and you lose one." These are invitations to imagine ourselves as part of the story! By doing so, you will experience Jesus as never before.

Jesus' stories are wonderful glimpses into characters not too unlike us. Jesus' tales include gardeners and farmers, cooks, vine keepers, and accountants. Yet, He also invites us to become princes/princesses, rich landowners, extravagant party givers, and even kings and queens. His parables often have remarkable endings as any good story does—a surprising twist that shocks us into seeing a remarkable truth we somehow missed because, quite frankly, we are too into ourselves.

We are to feel the emotions as if we were the one who lost something precious to us. We are to imagine what we would do if we found a priceless, hidden treasure. We are to envision that we have been beaten up, left to die in a ditch, praying for someone, anyone, to notice. And we are to ponder our feelings when we realize it's our worst enemy who helps us out.

Sometimes the surprise in Jesus' stories is who the hero turns out to be. Sometimes the hero is a money-grabbing tax man or an overly annoying neighbor. Sometimes it's a loving but misguided parent who raised a bratty kid who just squandered away a good chunk of the family fortune. And perhaps, Jesus intends for us to be His unlikely hero. You read that right. Perhaps, God wants us to love so much that we help the very person who ridicules us. Perhaps, God desires for us to listen and look for Him like we are in search of the finest pearl the world has ever known—even if taken for a fool.

My hope is that the parables can become a rich form of prayer for you. Yes, a story can be a prayer. Just what is prayer anyway? Saint John Damascene in the seventh century defined prayer as, "raising one's mind and heart to God." *Jesus Stories* will help you awaken your heart to love.

As you ponder each parable, I encourage you to listen for a message of hope or a challenge to grow. Most of all, my wish is for you to experience His love like never before. That is prayer!

It's true, we all love a good story. Jesus sure did. It's why He told so many of them with you in mind. Yes, Jesus meant His stories for you!

1

The Power of a Story

The shortest distance between a human being and the truth is a story. —*Anthony de Mello*

Jesus spoke all these things to the crowd in parables; He did not say anything to them without using a parable.

When the chief priests and the Pharisees heard Jesus' parables, they knew He was talking about them (Matt. 13:34, 21:45).

A story can be a powerful thing.

I love hearing stories of my mom. Why? I unfairly lost her at the tender age of six. For the most part, stories of her are all I have. I have precious few personal memories. So, stories of my mom mean the world to me.

Once, my brother and I were sharing memories of Mom. He would tell a memory, and I would try and top his with one of my own. I realized a lot of my "memories" are really stories passed on by my older siblings. It doesn't matter. They are mine now! We were soon lost in a world of storytelling. After some time and too many stories to count, someone listening in had enough and blurted out, "Okay, already, stop with how perfect your mom was! We get it!"

We all had a good laugh.

We went a tad overboard. Stories can do that. Stories can take you back to a special time and cause you to fall in love all over again. A story can change a heart. If you look at the time a person's beliefs have been profoundly changed, it is often because of a story that touched their emotions.[1] Here is an example. Let's remember David, one of the most admired biblical characters.

David is remembered in books, movies, and many other forms of art. Take Michelangelo's statue of David, maybe the most impressive sculpture we know. Towering seventeen feet high, the glistening white marble depicts an enviable physique of lean muscle any man would love as his own.

David is admired for good reason. As a mere boy, he was brave beyond compare, battling lions and bears to protect his sheep. He defeated a fierce enemy soldier no grown man was brave enough to fight, using a simple sling and a precise shot to his forehead. He played a mean harp. How cool is that! He was a singer and songwriter who penned half of the Psalms. As a man, he was a fierce warrior in battle. And to top it all off, he became king of a nation.

Yet, my favorite attribute of David is that he was "A man after God's own heart" (Acts 13:22). Wow. Think about that for more than a second. Don't most of us want to become a person with a pure and loving heart, a person as caring and compassionate as Christ? Maybe we wouldn't be the first to sign up for the dying-for-our-enemy part, but you get the idea.

Yes, David is admired for good reason. He had a heart *like* God and a heart *for* God. Unfortunately, David also had a heart for the ladies, and that got him in trouble. David slept with a beautiful yet married woman and had her husband killed in a cover-up operation. He slid from the heights of goodness to the depths of committing the nastiest of crimes.

David lived with the guilt of his horrid lapse in judgment. His secret must have gnawed deep in his soul!

How would God get through to David and stir his heart to repentance? What would God use to draw him back into intimacy, back to having a heart like God's?

God used a story. His friend, Nathan, told David (2 Samuel 12:1–7) a story of a poor man who owned a single lamb. The man deeply loved his lamb; it was more of a precious pet than livestock. He fed it his own food, let it drink from his own cup, and the lamb slept on his lap. A rich man with countless flocks of sheep took the poor man's only lamb and had it slaughtered for a guest just because he could.

As David heard this story, his imagination carried him away. He became furious. He angrily declared, "The rich man deserves to die!" As king, he could make that happen.

Nathan had him.

He told David, "You are the man! The man who deserves to die is you, David!" That is what finally broke David. He realized he was worse than the villain in the story. He blew it in real life. David admitted his guilt and humbly repented.[2]

Oh, the power of a story!

The power of a story is why great orators fill speeches with illustrations. It is why preachers use stories to drive home a point. It's why we enjoy telling stories to friends. Children don't say, "Tell me some facts." No, they want a story.[3] It's exactly why I love stories of my mom.

And guess what? The Bible is not only full of character stories; Jesus Himself *told* stories! He was an amazing Storyteller. His stories are called parables. Jesus tells His parables to stir our hearts. Notice I use the present tense, not the past? You see, Jesus still wants His stories to prick our emotions today just as they did for the eager listeners who gathered around Him long ago.

Madeleine L'Engle, a great storyteller herself, said, "Stories make us more alive, more human, more courageous, and more loving." Jesus wants to be alive and human for us today. Jesus tells parables to make us more courageous, more loving—maybe a little more like the repentant David.

Jesus was a Storyteller. Telling parables was one of Jesus' favorite forms of teaching. Scripture records around forty of them (depending on how you define a parable). About a third of Jesus' recorded teachings are parables.[4] A third! Parables have been defined as "earthly stories with a heavenly meaning."[5] Yet, that is not the best definition since they are meant to affect how we live in the present.[6] Jesus wants to touch our hearts in the here and now.

The Greek word for parable (*parabole*) meant a comparison, or at its root, "to throw alongside." Jesus threw a story alongside His teachings to wonderfully illustrate a point He wants us to see. If you studied algebra, you might remember the parabolic curve. A parabola is a curve that mirrors itself like the edge you would get if you cut through a bowl. Stories can act as a mirror. We are to see ourselves in the story, noticing something about us we did not know was there.

Perhaps you ignore the parables. They may seem strange and difficult to understand. Parables have been humorously described as part riddle, part joke, part fable, and totally unsolvable—maddening to the core. People have tried to neatly define what each one means so they are less mysterious, which is like trying to nail Jell-O to a tree![7]

I have found that if you approach a parable with a heart of wonder, they are not so complicated after all. By listening to them as a child would listen to a bedtime story, the meaning often jumps off the page straight into your heart! Often, it hits with a thud!

I firmly believe that Jesus didn't intend for His stories to be as difficult as we make them. It's why they are short and simple—profound for sure—yet simple. Once, while the disciples were scratching their heads, as confused over a parable as I was over calculus many years ago, He made this clear:

After He had left the crowd and entered the house, his disciples asked Him about this parable. "Are you so dull?" he asked. "Don't you see..." (Mark 7:17-18).

Parables are more easily understood when we realize they are metaphors from nature or everyday life, having an odd yet special appeal and drawing us through imagination to see a personal application (adapted from Dodd).[8] Let's use this as a working definition. Jesus used everyday people. He spoke of farmers, builders, fathers, mothers, and sons. He used everyday objects—seeds, rocks, soil, birds, yeast, and wine. Things we know. Things the ancient Hebrews knew very well.

If you wish to influence an individual or a group to embrace a particular value in their daily lives, tell them a compelling story. —Annette Simmons

Jesus' parables—appearing simple—were often profound weapons He used against his foes, almost like a stone and a sling.[9] When Jesus directed a parable to a specific individual, look out, that person was likely going to feel a thud of conviction![10] You and I are wonderfully brave to sit with a parable and invite Jesus to let us have it!

Jesus wants to incite our imagination; otherwise, He would not have told imaginative stories. It's that simple. A meaningful way to pray is to imagine Jesus speaking the parable just to you and listen for His words of love. Let yourself go. Jesus' parables are often chock full of humor and wit. Allow yourself to laugh. Allow yourself to even be the punch line!

Reading the parables was not meant to be a mysterious decoding exercise.[11] Just put yourself in the story and see what happens. Who are you drawn to in the story? Allow yourself to be the scoundrel. Funny how often it fits!

Let's be clear. Using your imagination is not making up what you hope the story means, nor is it using whimsical thoughts to produce a narrow perspective. I advocate first using basic interpretive know-how to determine its timeless message. Yet don't stop there. Allow the story to be what it is—a story. Allow it to come alive and change your heart like it did for David.[12]

Here is a profound thought. Jesus' life itself is like a parable.[13] He came alongside us to illustrate God. He joined the plot of God's great love story. In Jesus, God says, *Do you want to know what I am like? Let me be a story, the person of Jesus.* And with each parable, Jesus says, *Do you want to know how to live? Let me tell you a story.* Jesus told parables because He is a parable![14] He is Emmanuel, God with us.

But let's take it from the profound to the practical and see how your parable adventure will be structured. In each chapter, we will look at a single parable at a time. It will be a fun and heartwarming journey of listening.

Listening to the Story

In this section, we will interpret its message intended for you. The focus is to arrive at what the story meant to its original, first-century audience. Determining how they would have understood it is paramount if we are to hear its intended meaning for us. To understand any story told within a culture, one needs to understand that culture's social context and history.

We will look for the *primary* intent Jesus had in mind for telling it. Reducing the story to one major point is a curious endeavor, yet I believe by honing the message of the story into a single memorable truth, we are more likely to make it a part of our lives.

In the Appendix, I give concrete helps for interpreting the parables. Use it as a resource to sharpen your own interpretive skills.

Listening to the parables in this way is where to begin. Yet, I believe God invites you to go much deeper! He desires to speak to you in a way that pierces your heart and draws you ever closer to His infinite love.

Entering the Story

In this section, I describe my own experience of imaginative prayer, time spent listening to Jesus speaking the parable just for me. My hope is that by sharing my own experience, it will encourage you to have your own! You may be surprised at what you hear. Isn't that what we desire, to have a genuine relationship with the One who loves us the most?

Treating scripture in this fashion may be new for you. If so, the Appendix also has suggestions to help you engage in this wonderful practice.

Entering Jesus' stories in this manner will allow you to let go of your defenses and feel safe enough in God's embrace so you can hear Him speak. As a result, you are sure to fall in love with the Storyteller Himself.

Living the Story

In this section, you will be challenged to live out the message of the parable. There are questions for you to ponder. You may notice some recurring themes:

- Which character do you most relate to in the parable? Why?

- How do you see God's love in the parable? What does that mean to you?

- What is God inviting you to? What is He asking you to let go of?

A Blessing. Allowing the parables to touch our emotions and challenge our behavior takes work. Self-discovery is immensely meaningful work, but it is work, nonetheless. To soften the blow, if you will, I offer a prayer for you—a blessing to encourage you on your journey.

In addition, at the end of each chapter, look for the **Point of the Parable**, which sums up the message in a timeless, simple way.

Finally, a story is meant to be felt. And you can only feel a story by taking your time. Your journey through *Jesus Stories* will be most meaningful if you take it slow. His peculiar parables take time to fully grasp. Once grasped, they may be hard to accept.[15] A true journey of self-awareness takes time.

I highly recommend journaling your experience. Journaling helps the listening process flow, especially during imaginative prayer. Your journal will be a great source of reflection for later.

About two-thirds of Jesus' parables are found in Luke. Luke's parables are arranged within the travel narrative of Jesus.[16] For this reason, I focus on Luke's parables in the order He told them.

It is my intent to take you on a heartwarming journey with Jesus—to experience His wonderfully, quirky stories that will help you know God's love in a deeper way. This will be an exciting journey of listening. It has been said that listening is perhaps the greatest compliment one can give to another. Perhaps it's time to give Jesus that compliment.

I hope you will fall in love with His stories. More importantly, I hope you fall deeply in love with the Storyteller Himself, Jesus.

Be warned, His stories just may change you.

Oh, the power of a story!

2

In with the New

We cannot become what we want by remaining what we are. —Max Depree

He told them this parable: "No one tears a piece out of a new garment to patch an old one. Otherwise, they will have torn the new garment, and the patch from the new will not match the old. And no one pours new wine into old wineskins. Otherwise, the new wine will burst the skins; the wine will run out and the wineskins will be ruined. No, new wine must be poured into new wineskins. And no one after drinking old wine wants the new, for they say, 'The old is better'" (Luke 5:36–39).

Listening to the Story

We all enjoy new things. We also enjoy receiving or giving a gift to someone special. Yet, when it comes to matters of the heart, we settle for the way things are, the status quo. We tend to resist changing what we believe or how we act.

It was the same in the days of Jesus. He burst on the scene to usher in God's *new* kingdom. Yet, for the most part, everyone liked things the way they were. Sure, many were fascinated with His teachings. The hurting and the sick flocked to Jesus en masse for healing. Many people were in need, for medicine as we now know it did not exist in that day.

Everyone desperately wanted the ruthless Romans gone. But when it came to real change—changing their hearts—that was a different story. To genuinely change an attitude, behavior, or one's character takes real work. Not just anyone is up for the challenge. What precedes our first parable is a rather scrappy exchange between some Pharisees and Jesus.

But the Pharisees and the teachers of the law who belonged to their sect complained to his disciples, "Why do you eat and drink with tax collectors and sinners?" Jesus answered them, "It is not the healthy who need a doctor, but the sick. I have not come to call the righteous, but sinners to repentance." They said to him, "John's disciples often fast and pray, and so do the disciples of the Pharisees, but yours go on eating and drinking" (Luke 5:30–33).

The Pharisees. The religious elite of their day, the Pharisees, may have been the most content with the way things were. They had honed their how-to-live craft over countless generations, and they were fine with it, thank you very much!

The Pharisees could not fathom how a religious man could hang out with obvious riffraff. And you know what? Jesus let them know that the downtrodden is exactly who He came for!

The Pharisees retaliated by putting down Jesus and His disciples. They retaliated with ridicule, saying all Jesus and His disciples did was eat and drink! Can't you picture their condescending finger-wagging in the face of Jesus? What is hilarious is that the Pharisees never appreciated John the Baptist, but they sure used him to try and smear Jesus.

Ridiculing others is simply an attempt to feel superior. And all it shows is our own insecurities. Why would the Pharisees feel the need for ridicule? For one, they had a rigid, highly systemized faith. Pharisees fasted two days every week: Monday and Thursday. An everyday Jew was only expected to fast once a year, on the Day of Atonement.

Second, they prayed at set times every day: noon, 3 p.m. and 6 p.m.[1] They followed this ritual without exception. In their eyes, this was what a devout worshipper of God should do. It's as if they felt no one who is religious would ever eat on a fast day! Plain and simple. By pointing out that Jesus was eating on one of their fast days, they were gloating at just how special they were. I don't know about you, but I feel the need to stuff a finger down my throat.

The Parables. Jesus would have none of their ridicule and challenged their rigidity. Jesus told three mini "no one" parables of His own to make His point.

1. No one would ruin a brand-new garment by tearing a patch from it to put it on an old one. If so, you would end up ruining both! The Greek word *himation* refers to a finished upper garment, not simply cloth. It's as if Jesus was asking, "Would you buy a new shirt, cut it up to get a patch, and sew it onto an old one?" The answer is an emphatic and obvious, "No. No one would do that!"

2. No one would put new wine into an old wineskin. In Jesus' day, wine was initially fermented in clay pots. Then they would pour the wine into a wineskin for market. Sometimes they even did the fermenting in a large wineskin. After many uses, an old wineskin became brittle and would easily burst if used again for new-wine fermentation.

   Today, wine is fermented mostly in stainless steel tanks. Sometimes cement, wood, or ceramic is used. For aging, oak barrels are the vessel of choice since oak adds a wonderful flavor. Barrels are only used a few times. A barrel's ability to add flavor diminishes after a few uses. Put in today's terms, no modern winemaker would ever use an old oak barrel for aging new wine. It would be a waste of time.

3. After drinking old wine, no one wants the new stuff. It's not as good! After aging, the wine will be ready for consumption, but not before! Typically, wine is aged in barrels for one to two years to produce the intended results. No wine enthusiast would ever settle for new, unaged wine.

These three metaphors draw us into realizing that we like the old. We use old cloth to make a patch. In fact, we like to keep wearing old shirts. We like the feel of our favorite shirt. We prefer older, aged wine as opposed to the tart, raw taste of new, poorly aged wine.

These parables also draw us in for a final punch line without us realizing it. We think old is better! We prefer the tried and true. We feel a connection to it. It's what we know.

We like the *status quo*. The origin of this common expression comes from a longer Latin phrase, *in statu quo res erant ante bellum*, or "How things were before the war."[2] (That Latin phrase could be a fun one to try out on your friends!)

This entire phrase says a lot. It says that embracing new things is a bit like going to battle. That is so true, isn't it? Change is hard. We like things the way they are because who wants to engage in a fearful unknown? We fear the challenge and chaos of change. Fear is often the very thing that keeps us trapped in a cage of the way we have always been.

The Message. God is in the business of making all things new. God wants to break up your routine and teach you something wonderfully original! God wants us to experience a fresh batch of His love. God wants to burst open the cage that is holding us back.

The steadfast love of the Lord never ceases; His mercies never come to an end; they are new every morning (Lam. 3:22–23).

Here is a sad fact. Religious people tend to get stuck in the way things have always been.[3] Jesus is challenging you and me to want new mercies! Are we willing to listen for a new message of love from God every day? Or is our faith simply on autopilot?

Can you imagine if science or medicine never advanced in new thought and methods? I, for one, love my personal computer. I love that my house is fully heated for harsh Colorado winters. I love that I can take an antibiotic when I have a bacterial infection. I certainly appreciate the surgery I had that restored my youthful vision. These new things I now cannot imagine living without.

How about our spiritual lives? When is the last time Jesus did something completely new in your heart? Let's not, out of fear or apathy, say, "I'm fine the way I am." Let's not settle for what we've experienced with God up to now. Instead, let's seek out an exciting newness in our spiritual journey!

See, I am doing a new thing! Now it springs up; do you not perceive it? (Isaiah 43:19)

God desires to continually challenge us with newness, such as new ways of growing into His likeness and new ways of shedding our old self with all its baggage. The question remains, as it did in Isaiah's day, will we perceive it? Will we embrace it?

As you start your amazing journey with Jesus and ponder his marvelous parables, be ready for the new! Jesus will challenge your behavior, your attitude, and your motivation. It's no surprise that Jesus' first parable would be this one! It's as if Jesus is saying, "This is going to be an adventure of growth! Are you ready?"

God desires that we grow. He wants to give us a heart of genuine love. That often means doing the hard work of chiseling away at our ego. And it's a bit like going to battle.

I will give you a new heart (Eze. 36:26).

The irony of the parable is the punch line at the end. It's true that no one wants new wine when they can have perfectly aged, better-tasting old wine.

Yet, Jesus subtly compares Himself to new wine. Jesus suggested that the religious elite of His day were not ready for the tart taste of change He wanted to bring. They were happily stuck in their rigid ways like that old brittle wineskin.

What about us? Are we ready for change? Are we eager for Jesus? God desires an ever-growing, new heart for you!

Entering the Story

Look at me. I used to be a fisherman, and now I am a disciple of Jesus!

How lucky am I that the exciting new rabbi called me, a simple fisherman, as a disciple! Fishing was a trade I was proud of. After all night on the lake and a long morning of mending nets, I could go home with my tired head held high. It's an honest and respectable trade. Just the same, when Jesus asked me to follow Him, I dropped my nets on the spot and left everything behind. Why? It is an incredible honor to be a disciple of a rabbi. It's the dream of most every Hebrew boy.

Then, Jesus surprised the sandals off me. He asked Levi, a tax collector, to be a disciple! Are you kidding me? No honest, hardworking Galilean likes tax collectors. They take our hard-earned money and shuffle it to the Romans. Funny, every tax collector I know, and Levi is no exception, has a nice home and wears elaborate clothing. It's more than obvious they skim off money for themselves!

Now things are getting interesting. Levi, in celebration of his call to follow Jesus, throws a party at his house. He invites Jesus, us disciples, and all his tax collector friends. Some start to our spiritual journey with Jesus, I thought, partying with all these scoundrels!

Things got even crazier when some Pharisees show up. The scowls on their faces bellow out their obvious disapproval. They came to investigate this new, up-and-coming rabbi. To their delight, their skepticism proves correct. Jesus was not fasting as He should. Instead, He was feasting with hoodlums!

So, Jesus starts telling stories. The crowd is captivated. I know I sure am. Jesus walks over to Levi who was wearing a beautiful new cloak and says, "No one would be silly enough to cut a piece from this nice shirt..." Then walking over to me, He continues, "...and sew it on this old shirt," pointing to my dusty rag of a garment! Everyone chuckles, especially the rich tax collectors adorned in their fine robes. I feel a little embarrassed, but I must admit, I find it funny as well. Where is He going with this?

Jesus then gestures to the wine pourer who happens to be walking by with his wineskin strapped over his shoulder, and He says, "No one would pour new wine into an old brittle wineskin, for the skin would burst and the wine wasted." At that very moment, as if on cue, one of the guests is bumped, and he spills wine all over himself. Again, everyone chuckles.

Jesus then walks in front of a group of Pharisees and says, "No one, after drinking wonderfully aged wine, wants a new batch, saying, 'The old is far better.'" At that moment, you could hear a pin drop. Our minds are racing. Is Jesus saying the Pharisees are the old, and Jesus is the new? Is Jesus indirectly telling the Pharisees that they are stuck in their old crusty and wrong ways?

Jesus seems to be challenging the Pharisees to embrace His character and the way He reaches out and loves and accepts everyone. Jesus seems to say, "All you see in this room are people who don't measure up (to you). I see beautiful souls who need a friend and a Savior."

I am astounded at the courage of Jesus to confront the Pharisees! No one would do such a thing!

Then, Jesus walks over to me, rests his hand on my shoulder, and whispers, "What about you? Can you embrace the new? Can you walk with Me and accept new things I want to teach you?

"Sure Jesus," I blurt out with no hesitation.

Jesus continues, "Can you shed your hate and learn to love Levi?"

Jesus hit me with a sucker punch right in the gut that I was not expecting. I cannot believe He knew exactly what I was wrestling with. And it was true. Up to that point, when I looked at Levi, all I felt was hate.

"Yes, Jesus, I can. At least I want to try," I say.

Jesus looks at me with His glistening brown eyes and says, "I love you, My son. Let us embrace the new together."

Living the Story

What about us? Can we walk in newness this day? Can we seek a fresh experience of His love in our hearts?

The Lord's Prayer beautifully speaks of asking for just what we need each day. In the spirit of the Lord's Prayer, can we ask, "Father God, give me this day, a new heart of love."

I invite you to enter the story. Imagine yourself in the setting of the parable. Imagine the scene and Jesus speaking the parable just for you.

- Who do you gravitate to in the story? Do you resonate with a disciple, a tax collector, or a Pharisee? Why do you think you picture yourself as that character? How is God inviting you to change?

Point of the Parable:

Jesus wants to do a new thing in your heart.

We like new things. Yet, when it comes to matters of the heart, we like things the way they are.

Jesus said, "No one after drinking old wine wants the new unaged stuff."

Jesus is new. Taste and see how good new can be. Is it any wonder this is Jesus' first story?

- We all have subtle implicit biases that keep us doing the same old things. Be honest with yourself, what are yours? Ask God to show you.
- What are your prejudices God is asking you to abandon? Pray about ways you can be more aware of them. How can you experience Jesus' radical love today?

A Blessing for You, for Openness to Grow

May God quiet your heart with a fresh portion of love, like gently falling snow. May you enjoy His song of delight for you.

God desires for you to continually grow into His likeness. May you be open to embrace all the good and new things God has in store.

May you learn to notice and let go of your self-reliance—your consistent ways of attempting to patch up the pain in your heart. Instead, may you seek a new path of genuine healing and awakening to His love.

May you rejoice that God already sees you as wonderful. There is nothing you need to do to earn His love. It's already yours.

3

Eyes to See

If you judge people, you have no time to love them.
—Mother Teresa

Do not judge, and you will not be judged. Do not condemn, and you will not be condemned. Forgive, and you will be forgiven. Give, and it will be given to you. A good measure, pressed down, shaken together and running over, will be poured into your lap. For with the measure you use, it will be measured to you.

He also told them this parable: "Can the blind lead the blind? Will they not both fall into a pit? The student is not above the teacher, but everyone who is fully trained will be like their teacher.

"Why do you look at the speck of sawdust in your brother's eye and pay no attention to the plank in your own eye? How can you say to your brother, 'Brother, let me take the speck out of your eye,' when you yourself fail to see the plank in your own eye? You hypocrite; first take the plank out of your eye, and then you will see clearly to remove the speck from your brother's eye" (Luke 6:37–42).

Eyes to See

Listening to the Story

Are you blind?! People sometimes cruelly scream that out. Blindness itself is a cruel thing.

This parable may not speak as easily to us, for blindness is not as common today as it was in the first century. In the time of Jesus, blindness was sadly much more prevalent than in our western world today.

Babies born today receive antiseptic eye drops (Erythromycin) as a matter of course. This has its roots in the late 1800's.[1,2] In the ancient world, infants could easily develop eye infections (Ophthalmia) from unsanitary conditions that could lead to blindness. Cataracts, glaucoma, and other eye diseases can also cause blindness and were common. It has been estimated that, in antiquity, perhaps a tenth of the population of rural villages in Palestine may have been blind.[3] A tenth!

The only recourse a blind person had in antiquity was to have someone lead them around. For, without a guide, a blind person was utterly helpless.

Today, we have plenty of real-life stories of blind people accomplishing amazing things. Marla Runyan was a world-class runner and a 2000 USA Olympian. Yet, Marla is legally blind. Dereck Rabelo is an accomplished Brazilian surfer, yet blind. In 2011, Mark Anthony Riccobono took the wheel of a Ford and drove solo around the Daytona International Speedway. Riccobono is blind. Christopher Downey is an architect, planner, and consultant who lost his sight after a tumor wrapped around his optic nerve. Erik Weihenmayer is blind yet has climbed staggering peaks and kayaked the waters of the Grand Canyon.

Most amazing to me is Pete Eckert, an award-winning, successful blind photographer. How does a blind man take photographs? He visualizes the image he wants to create in his mind and uses his senses of sound, touch, and memory to take a photograph. Pete likes to say, "I am a visual person. I just can't see."

Back in Jesus' day, I am not sure there were similar opportunities for the blind.

A Sandwich. What is so fascinating is that Jesus sandwiched his blind-leading-the-blind parable between two teachings on judging. At first glance, we may think there is nothing to this. I think this is extremely significant! It's as though Jesus is saying when we judge, we may as well be blind.

And that is the remarkable truth Jesus knew—that very often, when we judge, the thing we are critical of in others is the very thing we are guilty of ourselves! We simply don't see it. Blind to our own faults, yet we project those same faults onto others.

Every time I judge someone else, I reveal an unhealed part of myself. —*Anonymous*

In the first teaching, the top slice of the judge sandwich, if you will, Jesus gives us two things to not do and two things to do. Do not judge. Do not condemn. These are the two don'ts. He then says, forgive and give, and you will be forgiven and given to. Forgiving and giving are the two things to do. The high-level message here is, how we treat others is how we will be treated. But it goes deeper than that.

The words used by Jesus brilliantly explain the inner workings of judging—what happens in our subconscious thoughts or attitude when we judge. Let's look and see.

The word for judge (*krino*) used by Jesus here literally means to separate or to make a distinction between. In our minds, we are separating out those who we do not think measure up...to us! We take it further and condemn those whom we have separated out. In our minds, we sentence them as unworthy! We are being exceedingly cruel to each other without even realizing it.

I like what Jesus said about judging: "Don't do it!" Quit it! Stop It! Nothing subtle about that advice, is there? It has been said that you can reduce all of Jesus' entire teachings into two little words, *don't judge.* I think that might be spot on.

Jesus taught us to not judge on other occasions. Jesus said, "God did not send his Son into the world to condemn the world, but to save the world" (John 3:17). Jesus said, "You judge by human standards; I pass judgment on no one. But if I do judge, my decisions are true" (John 8:15-16). And on the cross when He had every reasonable right to judge those who unfairly beat him and strung him up to suffer in the most miserable way, He instead asked God to forgive them.

Now, I need to carefully make a distinction here. As humans, we need to make judgments, to discern what is helpful or harmful for us and our family. Paul, in 1 Corinthians 2:15 said, "The person with the Spirit makes judgments about all things." But notice the focus is on *things* and not *people*. There is a deep chasm of difference between making wise decisions and condemning people in our minds!

What about the two things we are to do? We are to forgive (*apolyo*), which literally means to set free! I love that, don't you? We are to stop the downward spiral of judging and condemning, and in-

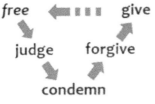

stead, set others free through forgiving and giving! That is powerful.

I like to view these words and the pattern this way. Before we judge, there is freedom. There is freedom both we and the other person enjoy. Once we judge, we toss the other person in our minds' jail cell of less than we are. Freedom is lost. We send them into bondage even further as we condemn them as guilty in our minds.

It's as though we chain them up, put them behind bars, and throw away the key. That is the inner workings of judging. Instead, let's set them free! Let's open that jail cell. And here is a beautiful truth—when we set them free, we free ourselves as well! We free ourselves from the ongoing torment of holding on to a grudge.

Now, let's get back to that judge sandwich. For the bottom bun, Jesus' humor takes center stage. Why do you look at a little *speck* in another's eye when you have a *plank* in yours? That is downright funny! I personally enjoy woodworking. So, I know firsthand the pain that a mere speck of sawdust can cause in my eye. It kills! Now, picturing myself trying to get a speck out of your eye while I have a two-by-four plank in my eye? That's funny. Yet, it's also sad.

To put it a different way, we can only criticize others when we ourselves are completely free of faults. But you and I both know what that means. We will never have a right to criticize![4] Plain and simple.

I mentioned previously that when we judge others, most often, we are guilty of the very same thing. Modern psychology calls this *projection*. Projection is an unhealthy defense mechanism whereby I ignore the crud in myself yet see it in you. Here is how it works. If a certain characteristic in another person really annoys you, there is a good chance you have that very same characteristic buried within yourself! You just don't see it, or you wish you didn't. The source is often an early emotional wound or an unhealthy overcompensation in your heart.

Easy to judge the mistakes of others, difficult to recognize our own mistakes. —*Anonymous*

I love it that Jesus taught us what modern psychology took a while to figure out!

The Message. Oh, the power of this Jesus story. When we judge others, we are blind to our own needs, shortcomings, or weaknesses. And the result is falling into a pit. A pit of ego. A pit of resentment. A pit of hypocrisy.

Our world today tends to be very dualistic—the idea that something is either good or bad with no in-between. You believe and stand for either this view or that view. Pick a side and let's verbally duke it out. And oh, how we criticize, judge, and condemn those on the other side! We fail to realize there may be a hundred or a thousand degrees of subtle variation in between.[5]

We think we have it all figured out, so we point out the other's failures and faults to somehow confirm that we are right. We need to realize it is okay, even beautiful, to allow for a bit of mystery in our life! We do not need to have all the answers.

Why has Christianity earned the reputation of being exclusionary, judgmental, and hypocritical? Sadly, it is because that is the role we often play. Let's reverse this pattern of exclusionary Christianity.

The self-righteous scream judgments against others to hide the noise of skeletons dancing in their own closets. —John Mark Green

Who do you tend to judge? Who do you condemn? Spend time with God asking Him to show you. You may be surprised to see what is buried within you.

Are you blind? At times we may be mad enough to think or say that to another. More importantly, we need to prayerfully ask ourselves: Where am I bind? What am I blind to? Asking God to show you your blind spots may hurt a little, but freeing yourself from the shackles of bitterness will give you a joy you have never known!

Entering the Story

I have been captivated by Jesus, the new rabbi from our own region of Galilee. Nothing significant ever comes from Galilee is the slander we always hear. Yet, here is Jesus from lowly Nazareth whom everyone from mighty Jerusalem is flocking to see.

One day, He worked his way to a hillside, which sloped down

to the shores of our mighty Lake Tiberias. We disciples sat next to Jesus, and the other followers found spots on the slope to sit and hear Him speak. What would He share today? We couldn't wait to find out. As a new disciple, I couldn't be more excited. I must admit, I felt special to be handpicked by Jesus and to have a first-hand, seat next to Him.

As He taught that morning, it all began to make sense, or so I thought. I could not help but notice everyone else's imperfections. I noticed the bum legs, the people riddled with disease, and the bad behavior in those around me. I brashly thought to myself, *I can sure see why Jesus picked me as a disciple and not them.* There were even several blind people. I felt so sorry for them. *No way they could ever be a disciple,* I thought to myself.

The teaching of Jesus that morning was amazing. It was all about loving others, even our enemies. Jesus taught that we could be happy even if we are poor, meek, or hungry. Jesus spoke such penetrating and challenging words. I was somehow still caught up in looking around at the crowd. I wondered how they would react to His words.

Then, Jesus looked my way and told a story with words that cut straight to my heart. His teaching went to the very thing I was doing—judging, criticizing, and condemning! I realized what I had been doing. It stung! I felt exposed and worse than trash. Yet, the love I felt from Jesus at that moment was so strong. Jesus' face spoke love to my wounded heart.

I suddenly understood that Jesus did not pick me because I am somehow better than most. Far from it! Jesus handpicked me to transform me. He wants me to grow and to change. He wants me to learn to love everyone the same on that mountainside—just as Jesus wonderfully loves us all.

And here is also what I now realize. I am the blind one! That's right. I am full of blind spots. And Jesus wants me to see. Jesus wants to expose all my prejudices and make me a new person.

I have so much to learn, Jesus. Thank you for picking me to follow You!

Then Jesus leaned toward me and whispered in my ear, saying, "Remember the old proverb, 'The camel cannot see its own hump?'"

"But don't worry, I will help you see it," He said.

Jesus walked away, looking back at me with a wink and a smile that communicated, "I love you!"

Living the Story

We all have biases, prejudices, and pre-conceptions we may not see. Early-life influences and events helped to shape these in us. Greater awareness of our biases is a critical first step for spiritual growth.

Someone may have hurt you badly, and you may be hanging onto that hurt. It may feel like they do not deserve your forgiveness. Jesus invites you to set them free. By doing so, you will be free as well.

Point of the Parable:

What annoys you in others is often the very thing you are guilty of yourself.

It is so easy to see the faults in others while being blind to our own. Judging only imprisons us in a cell of discontent.

Jesus said, "Take the wood plank out of your own eye. Ignore the speck in others."

Jesus desires to heal the hurts in our hearts and for us to enjoy the freedom of forgiveness.

- Imagine Jesus having a conversation with you about judging others. What does Jesus say to you?

- Be honest. Who do you tend to judge? What actions can you take to stop your habit of judging?

- Take some time and identify what you tend to project onto

others. When does it occur? What hurt resides deep in your heart that influences you?

A Blessing for You, for an Awakening to See

May Jesus, who did not condemn but embraced the hurting, the broken, and the wounded, extend the same non-judgmental love to you. May you realize He sees everything about you, blind to nothing, yet loves you deeply.

May God grant in you a desire to see your own blind spots. May you allow God to reveal the planks of ego within yourself that need to be peeled away. May you slow down, listen, and allow God's Spirit to gently penetrate your heart and to reveal what is buried inside.

As you notice your own hidden biases, may you take the journey towards freedom and see others with kindness and with understanding.

4

Digging Deep

What you are is God's gift to you. What you become is your gift to God. —Hans Urs Von Balthasar

"Why do you call me, 'Lord, Lord,' and do not do what I say? Everyone who comes to me and hears my words and acts on them, I will show you whom He is like. He is like a man building a house, who dug deep and laid a foundation on the rock; and when a flood occurred, the torrent burst against that house and could not shake it, because it had been well built.

"But the one who has heard and has not acted accordingly is like a man who built a house on the ground without any foundation; and the torrent burst against it and immediately it collapsed, and the ruin of that house was great" (Luke 6:46–49).

Listening to the Story

A friend told me about her path to recovery after a severe accident. She was regularly going to the doctor yet not getting better. The doctor knew why. He rather brashly told her to never come back unless she would do what he said! That was the wakeup call she needed. She changed course and did everything he asked and guess what? She got better.

In this parable, Jesus' words are a bit like the doctors. Do not call me Lord unless you do what I say!

The parable is set at the end of the Sermon on the Mount. Jesus seems to say, "I just gave you a synopsis of how to live, so now do it!" Let's remember the main teachings of his great sermon, the full extent of which is in Matthew's gospel.

Jesus spoke on godly character (the Beatitudes), honest living ("You have heard it said..."), living a life of love (for enemies and the needy), praying and fasting, and sincerity of heart. It is a beautiful discourse on having a heart for God and others. Jesus concludes with a simple message, "Now go and live it!" So, to help drive this point home, He tells a story.

A Foundation. Jesus uses a building illustration and makes use of the geography of Palestine. Some riverbeds within the deserts of Palestine are completely dry and sandy most of the time. A *wadi* (wah-dee), as riverbeds are called in Arabic, can have nearby trees with roots reaching deep to water beneath the stark, dry surface. These flat spots with a nice shade tree or two may seem like a great building site, but you couldn't pick a poorer place to build!

In the rainy season, the wadis can become engulfed in flashes of rapidly moving water, washing away most anything in their path.[1] I have driven in a dry wadi in the Sinai of Egypt and seen a car washed up on a bank, twenty feet above the riverbed. It had been lodged at that great height by the current from a seasonal torrential downpour.

Jesus, as a carpenter, knew a thing or two about foundations. As He often did in his parables, Jesus crafted an imaginative story from His own experiences. Jesus more than likely dug a few foundations as a builder.[2] I enjoy picturing Jesus telling carpenter stories!

The best homes in ancient Palestine were built of stone.

28

Modern excavations indicate that homes were often constructed of one or two levels of rough masonry, with foundations cut into solid rock. This formed a rock-solid base, even if the upper floor was made of more fragile mud bricks.[3]

A rock foundation would have been a familiar spiritual metaphor as well.

"See, I lay a stone in Zion, a tested stone, a precious cornerstone for a sure foundation; the one who relies on it will never be stricken with panic" (Isaiah 28:16).

And, of course, a rock is used as a symbol for God Himself many times in scripture.

The Lord is my rock, my fortress and my deliverer; my God is my rock, in whom I take refuge (Psalm 18:2).

But here is the thing—digging a deep foundation takes a lot of work with seemingly little to show for it. I watched several high-rise buildings go up in downtown Denver back in the 80s. I marveled at the large construction projects from my office window. For the tallest buildings, it took what seemed like forever to dig deep foundations. The taller the building, the deeper they dug.

The Message. What was Jesus' message to His disciples and to us? In short, intimacy with God is the foundation needed to weather life's storms. After teaching incredible words on living a life of love and what that life looks like, Jesus says to do it. In essence, Jesus is saying to *be* love. And the only chance we have of being a loving person is to be a person of prayer.

Wait a minute, you might be thinking. How do you conclude that a parable about *doing* what Jesus says relates to *being* a person of intimacy? The key is the context. In both Luke and Matthew, the parable is recorded immediately following Jesus' words on a tree and its fruit. Jesus says that only a good tree produces good fruit. Jesus wants us to be genuine.

It is not the mountain we conquer, but ourselves.
—Sir Edmund Hillary

In Matthew 7:21–23, there are even clearer clues. Jesus tells of people who are consumed with doing great things (prophesying, driving out demons, and performing miracles) and thinking that is the surefire way of entry into His presence. Jesus says their only fault is He did not *know* them. Our relationship with God is vitally more important than our performance. You might want to read that again and allow it to sink in. We are to know Jesus, and knowing Him only comes through a life of prayerfully being with Him.

In Matthew's version of the Sermon on the Mount, when Jesus discusses prayer, He says to "Go into your room, close the door, and pray" (Matt. 6:6). A sincere and consistent prayer life is the key for developing a heart for God. Getting alone with God and doing more listening than talking is the spade needed for digging a deep relationship with Him.

It sometimes can feel like work to pray, especially when seeking a changed heart. It can feel like digging into rock-hard dirt. Richard Foster gives us the key, "Real prayer comes not from gritting our teeth but from falling in love."

In the spring of 2018, my wife and I were given news that sucker-punched us in the gut. She was diagnosed with stage 3, ovarian cancer. It felt like a torrent of water raging down a riverbed headed straight for us. And there was no outrunning it. *This is what happens to other people,* we thought!

Many things helped us cope with the surgeries and months of nasty chemotherapy, namely incredible support from family and friends. Yet, what I witnessed firsthand in my wife was nothing short of remarkable. She had a strength, an unwavering trust, and an unexplainable peace, knowing her God had it under control. She did everything asked of her by the doctors and gently let God do the healing work.

How was she able to do this? My wife had built a bedrock of

intimacy with God that she had consistently dug, morning after morning, throughout her life. This enabled her to never doubt the love of her Savior. She could endure the pain and uncertainty with a gentleness and grace I had never seen before. It was a result of her deep foundation of spending time with God in prayer.

So many people build their lives on shallow things. They settle for less than intimacy with God. When life is going smoothly, they feel and look rock solid.[4] But, looking good is not what counts.[5] What we need is a genuine faith that can handle the rough stuff.

Life will get tough. And it is often times of suffering that can draw us to God and encourage remarkable growth. Yet the suffering will also show us our underlying intimacy with God or lack thereof. Intimacy with God helps us through the rough stuff. It is the ultimate chicken-and-egg, which came first conundrum.

We need to do what Jesus says! And what Jesus says is to love God with all our hearts—to have God be the highest priority in our life. That is no small order, friends! It only happens through consistent time with Him in prayer. It takes time listening. It takes consistent times of yielding. Yet, as Oswald Chambers once said, "Once the joy of intimacy with God has been experienced, life becomes unbearable without it!" Once we taste how wonderful time with God is, we cannot get enough.

Do you consistently enjoy time with God in your own sacred place of prayer? What keeps you from time with Him? You may want to ask God how to dig a deeper foundation into Him and His character.

It's doctors' orders! We just need to do it.

Entering the Story

I am a young man, a boy really, from Galilee. My father is a builder. So, of course, I work alongside my father and am learning the trade. I have much to learn, yet I love the thought of running the business myself someday.

We have taken on a new project that we are extremely excited about. We are building a new synagogue for our village! Building a special place of prayer is thrilling, to say the least. Our old synagogue was just that—old and in disarray. We want our new synagogue to last for centuries! We want to build it well. And that requires digging a deep and solid foundation!

We are digging the foundation and the work never seems to end! We dig and dig and dig some more. Just when I think we might be deep enough, my father inspects the soil. He picks up some dirt, filters it through his fingers, and blurts out what we all fear, "Keep digging boys. We need to find bedrock."

Today I took a small break from that hard work to hear Jesus speak. What a nice change from all that digging! I was a little frustrated that my father put me on the digging crew! *What a menial job for the son of the boss,* I thought! I also need a break from the other guys on the crew. We have our fair share of disagreements.

Today, I lost my temper and shouted at a fellow worker. Something I did more often than I'd like to admit. I guess I want the guys to respect me, and that's how it comes out sometimes.

But as Jesus speaks, I forget about all that. Jesus captivates my heart with His words. Jesus teaches on loving others and how to treat them. How convicting was that!

Then, crazy enough, He spoke of a wise builder who built on a rock. I almost chuckled. I also thought of the words from the Torah referring to God as my Rock! I love those words.

It started to make sense. Just as we need a firm foundation of bedrock for the synagogue, so it lasts for centuries, I need God's love to be at the center of my heart!

I must prayerfully allow God to change my tendency toward anger and to soften my heart. I need a love for the guys on the crew. I also need to gladly take whatever job Dad gives me!

A sincere heart of love is deep within me. I know it! Father God let's unearth it together. Let's find it. Please strip away the layers of false self I have built up instead. Please peel away these faulty layers that are covering up my heart of love.

I was excited to get back to the job site. I wanted to find bedrock! I dug the rest of that week with more vigor. It was exciting when I heard the unmistakable ping of my pickax hitting solid rock.

I am also excited to continue my steady job of digging deep into God's love. That is my daily prayer.

After all, I am the son of a builder. And God desires to build me into a genuine man of love.

Living the Story

Read through the Sermon on the Mount both in Matthew (chapters 5-7) and in the shorter version in Luke (6:17-45). Spend time soaking up Jesus' words. Use this as a backdrop before enjoying our parable.

Jesus invites you to let go of needless ways in which you seek to get ahead or get noticed. What do you do that you often later regret? Perhaps, you talk too much and listen too little, or you are much too critical of others. Do you spend too much time thinking of only yourself?

- Put yourself into the story. Invite Jesus to tell you where you have been foolish, and you did not see it.

- Recall a time in your life when you glided through a rough event as a result of your rock-solid faith in God. Think back on

Point of the Parable:

Intimacy with God is the foundation needed to weather life's storms.

We often know what to do, we just don't do it.

Jesus said, "Build your life on the solid foundation of listening and yielding to God, your Rock."

Now that is something to build on!

33

how God graciously met your needs. Thank Him for that special time.

• Consider practically how you can enhance your personal prayer time. Can you develop a sacred place of your own? Can you find a better time to be with God? Try and increase the amount of time you spend simply listening to God. Learn the joy of speaking less and listening more for His words of love.

A Blessing for You, as You Dig Deep into God's Love

May you drop any guilt you feel from not having enough solitary times with God. Instead, may you feel only gratitude that God desires time with you. He is always near to you.

May God develop in you a heart that enjoys His presence. May you create a sacred place in your home that you and God can share together.

May you dig deep, developing a relationship with Jesus that is as solid as granite. May you allow God to speak words of love to you in your times together. Take time to listen.

May you feel His love. May you enjoy His love. May you radiate His love.

5

Better Than Bad

I think the drug of choice these days is knowing we're better than.   —Nadia Bolz-Weber

When the Pharisee who had invited him saw this, he said to himself, "If this man were a prophet, he would know who is touching him and what kind of woman she is— that she is a sinner."

Jesus answered him, "Simon, I have something to tell you." "Tell me, teacher," he said.

"Two people owed money to a certain moneylender. One owed him five hundred denarii, and the other fifty. Neither of them had the money to pay him back, so he forgave the debts of both. Now which of them will love him more?" Simon replied, "I suppose the one who had the bigger debt forgiven." "You have judged correctly," Jesus said.

Then He turned toward the woman and said to Simon, "Do you see this woman? I came into your house. You did not give me any water for my feet, but she wet my feet with her tears and wiped them with her hair. You did not give me a kiss, but this woman, from the time I entered, has not stopped kissing my feet. You did not put oil on my head, but she has poured perfume on my feet. Therefore,

I tell you, her many sins have been forgiven—as her great love has shown. But whoever has been forgiven little loves little."

Then Jesus said to her, "Your sins are forgiven." The other guests began to say among themselves, "Who is this who even forgives sins?" Jesus said to the woman, "Your faith has saved you; go in peace" (Luke 7:39–50).

Listening to the Story

"I can do it myself." That tends to be the motto of a toddler. I know, I raised two sons and have three wonderful granddaughters. Yet, as an adult, I'm not much different. I still think I can do most everything myself. This parable speaks of this very attitude.

For this parable, we have the complete story. We have an incident that causes a ruckus. We have Jesus telling a parable to explain the scandalous behavior and then explaining just who the scoundrel really was! With all these elements, we have a fighting chance at deciphering Jesus' intent.

The event which led to Jesus' parable is an amazing contrast between a man who thought he had everything figured out with a woman who knew very well she was a train wreck. I admire that train wreck of a woman. She had great self-awareness. Most of us need an awakening. Most people spend a lifetime reacting to situations—sleepwalking through life—instead of acting in ways true to who they really are.

The Setting. Jesus accepts a dinner invitation from Simon, a Pharisee. Pharisees were the religious cream-of-the-crop of their day. We do not know the intentions of Simon, but it appears he was more than a little skeptical, yet inquisitive. He wanted to evaluate the validity of Jesus for himself. It is remarkable that Jesus would walk into this kind of situation. It is a bit like a boy walking right into a circle of bullies and asking, "What's up, guys?" Jesus desired to reach everyone, even the skeptical, so walk smack dab in the middle of the bullies He did.

As was the custom, dinner was probably in an outer courtyard and the uninvited would often show up as onlookers to listen in and crash the party.[1]

A woman who seemed to be the village harlot suddenly took center stage by traipsing in and displaying less-than-modest affection toward Jesus. It must have been a little embarrassing to the other guests. She cried at Jesus' feet, uncovered her hair to use as a makeshift towel, and then gently massaged his feet with expensive perfume. The remarkable thing is it wasn't embarrassing to Jesus at all—He knew how to give and receive extravagant love.

The Customs. The woman who could not contain her love acted in at least three outlandish ways. A proper woman would never show her hair in public. Kissing another's feet was the ultimate way to show honor. It displayed deep humility and affection yet was rarely done.[2] Anointing feet with costly perfume would have been extravagant at the least and maybe even offensive.[3] Why? The perfume could have been what she used in her trade. Need I say more?

This was when Simon the Pharisee had seen enough. In disgust, he said to himself, "If this man were a prophet, he would know exactly who is touching him and what kind of woman she is." Jesus did not pass Simon's test. He must be a fraud. Jesus was found guilty in the court of Simon. So, Simon and his bully buddies verbally abused Jesus.

Jesus knew very well the kind of woman who was dousing his feet in tears and perfume. Jesus also knew what Simon was thinking, so He told him a story which He cleverly had Simon himself solve. It was a bit like a knock-knock joke. And guess who the joke was on? What we need to realize is that Simon disrespected Jesus even before the ridiculing began. How? It was customary to greet an honored guest with a kiss and to provide water for them to wash their feet. In addition, sometimes, one would even sprinkle a little perfume on a guest's head.[4] These things are what you did for someone you loved or respected. Simon offered none of these to Jesus. He seemed more caught up in the fanfare of the evening, neglecting to show proper respect to his guest.

In an amazing contrast, the woman, who in no way was the host, acted the part. She sat at Jesus' feet and could not hold back her love. She was moved to tears. She saw Jesus was worth every bit of her costly perfume. To the woman, no one else was even there—it was just Jesus and her! She emptied her jar of perfume. Neither could her love for Jesus be contained.

Her behavior was outrageous, and Simon was beside himself. So, Jesus told a parable of two forgiven debts. A contrast in the amount of debt and appreciation. A contrast to make a point.

I wonder if Simon understood that he was a character in the parable. He probably initially didn't, so Jesus made sure he did with His explanation. It was His way of rubbing salt in Simon's wound.

Jesus asked Simon, "Do you see this woman?" This very question is riddled with intrigue. Sure, Simon saw her. She was the reason he was so bent out of shape! Yet did he really see her? He noticed everything about her that bothered him. He saw her as despicable. Sirach 26:22 (Apocrypha) refers to prostitutes as "spittle." Simon saw her as nasty spit and not a beautiful, forgiven person full of love. He did not truly see her. Far from it.

Simon also didn't see himself honestly. He didn't see his own need for forgiveness. She had sins galore, but he had a mountain full of ego! And he was somehow blind to that mountain.

The Message. The obvious message in Jesus' parable is "The one who is forgiven more loves more." Yet, on a deeper level, Jesus uses this event to contrast two vastly different approaches in life, self-sufficiency versus self-awareness. Let's look at the difference.

- **Self-sufficiency.** We are good at what we do, and we know it. We have little need for help. We are the center of our world because, quite frankly, we can stand on our own. In the words of the 1980s song, "It's hard to be humble when you're perfect in every way."

- **Self-awareness.** We know our strengths, but we also are aware of our faults. We understand our behavioral patterns. We realize when we need help, and we seek it out. We are honest with God. We are grateful for help. Our love is extravagant and hard to contain.

You're a soul made by God, made for God, and made to need God, which means you were not made to be self-sufficient. —Dallas Willard

I believe this is what Jesus intended both Simon and all of us to see. Our own self-sufficiency keeps us from intimacy. Jesus wanted Simon to see that his faults may not have seemed as bad as the harlot's, but that he still had plenty of needs. Simon was the person of smaller character in this story. Why? He was entirely too self-absorbed, self-centered, and too concerned with pointing out her failures. Simon did not know how to see the beauty in others. And Simon did not realize any debt he had was a debt he in no way could pay!

An ugly truth is that we like to think there are degrees of sin. And we like to qualify who commits the worst ones. Sadly, we feel a tad taller if we cut others down to size.

We must be willing to embrace everyone, faults and all. The only thing that holds us back from embracing others is the simple fact that we feel we are better. Ouch! We think we are better than bad. We aren't! We are all equally in need of God's love and forgiveness.

Self-sufficiency is the enemy of salvation. If you are self-sufficient, you have no need of God. If you have no need of God, you do not seek Him. If you do not seek Him, you will not find Him. —*William Nicholson*

Yet, there are layers of love! We can love the lovely. That's easy. At least, at times. We can love the ones who desperately need it. That is harder! The only way to love the unlovable is to let go of our ego and soak in God's infinite love for us.

And this, my friends, we cannot do by ourselves. We need God's immeasurable grace.

I guess I can't do it myself, after all.

Entering the Story

I suppose I want both. I want to believe in this new Rabbi Jesus, but I also love the security of being a well-respected spiritual guide. I worked so hard early in life memorizing the Torah, developing a firm grip of spiritual truth, and attaining the status of Pharisee.

I must admit, though, I am attracted to the freedom that the disciples of Jesus seem to enjoy. His teachings are so pure and fresh and make my heart skip with excitement.

So, I decided to invite Jesus to my house and see and observe Him for myself. So much preparation is involved in hosting a meal with a guest such as Jesus. With his popularity, having Jesus for a meal means having the entire village.

Being a stickler for details, I was consumed with ensuring we would have enough space, food, and entertainment. I suppose I wanted to impress Jesus. I was also hoping we could engage in enough spiritual dialogue so I could judge for myself if He might be a prophet as some say He is. I wanted to know. We all do!

I was so caught up in getting ready, Jesus arrived before I could greet Him at the door. Hopefully, my servants provided Him with water for His feet and an honorable greeting.

Soon we were reclining at the table and a lively discussion was underway. I could see Jesus was so completely at peace with who He was. He was humble yet confident. He started asking me questions, and I was happy to engage in a little spiritual debate. That is what we Jews do! The evening was everything I had hoped for, that is, until she came!

Why is the town harlot here? I wondered. *What an embarrassment! How can a woman so full of sin show herself in public? Has she no shame?* She went directly to Jesus' feet, and in full display of everyone, she anointed them with perfume from around her neck. We all know that's probably the very perfume she uses to freshen up her clients. How disgusting!

I concluded at that very moment that Jesus must be a fake. As priests, we must keep ourselves pure. For Jesus to allow that sinful woman to touch Him and caress His feet was despicable. It was hard to watch.

Jesus said He had something to tell me. I couldn't wait to hear how He would try and justify this! Instead, Jesus told me a story.

He told a story of two people who owed money. Neither could repay, yet both were graciously forgiven their debt. Jesus asked me to solve His riddle of which debtor would most appreciate having their debt forgiven. With satisfaction I gladly solved it.

I felt satisfied when Jesus said I was right. The words He then spoke, however, made me feel anything but right. He pointed out my neglect as a host. I had failed to give Jesus a greeting, a kiss, water, or perfume. And how this despicable woman (my thoughts, not His) had done what I failed to do. That hurt!

Jesus then told me He would forgive me, if only I would let Him. Jesus knows me all too well. By His look, I somehow can tell He knows my fears are what drive me to please and perform. He knows I enjoy this holy image I display. He knows I hide my own wounds and shortcomings behind my impressive priestly robes. He even knows of the times I had gazed at this very woman's beauty and undressed her in my mind.

Jesus then told me I could learn to love as well if I could only admit my need for forgiveness. I wanted to be a person of love, to be free from the shackles of this fake persona. Yet, there was safety in who I was. Jesus wanted me to surrender my façade. I wanted both.

As a priest, I too had a small jar of oil I used in prayer to anoint others. It felt as though my heart was being ripped open. A part of me wanted to bend down, anoint his feet all over again with my oil, to show my love for Him and to now honor Jesus.

A part of me wanted to. I felt such torment as I realized it would take a humbleness I didn't have. Inside I was a wreck, and I simply couldn't give up all that I knew.

I couldn't. I simply couldn't. That night I cried.

Living the Story

Read through the event that triggered Jesus telling the story of the two debtors. There is the stoic, had-it-all-together Pharisee. There is the hard-to-watch woman overflowing with love and gratitude.

- Put yourself into the story. Would you be Simon or the woman? Or would you be a bystander full of wonder? Why do you think you gravitated to that character?

- It has been said, "I've never seen a smiling face that wasn't beautiful." How does that resonate with you? Do

Point of the Parable:

What keeps us from genuine intimacy is our own stubborn self-sufficiency.

"I can do it myself" is often our motto.

Jesus said, "Whoever is most aware of their own needs will most embrace My love."

We do not love because we think we are better than.

you tend to notice the beauty in others or their faults? Are you naturally skeptical and judgmental, or accepting? Spend time asking God to enable you to genuinely see the beauty in others.

- In a very real way, Jesus comes to your house for a dinner party every day! Can you be extravagant in appreciation that He wants to be a part of your life? How will you spend today with Jesus?

A Blessing for You on Your Self-awareness Journey

May you hear Jesus' gentle words, "I see you. I love you." May you become more aware of Love Himself pouring His fragrance of complete acceptance over you. There is no earning it. There is no risk of losing it.

May you see with new eyes the overflowing, limitless, extravagant love that God pours out. May this open your heart to simply receive His love, and may you be filled with joy throughout this day.

As you experience His genuine love, which far surpasses our cheap self-centered love, may you be filled with the courage to grow in self-awareness. May God grant in you a desire to notice your ways of reacting that are an attempt to protect or hide the real you. May you have the courage to ask for help, ask for forgiveness, and be truly vulnerable when needed.

May you break open the flask and see the sacred beauty in others.

6

Sower and Soil

Minds are like parachutes—they only function when open. —*Thomas Dewar*

While a large crowd was gathering and people were coming to Jesus from town after town, He told this parable: "A farmer went out to sow his seed. As He was scattering the seed, some fell along the path; it was trampled on, and the birds ate it up. Some fell on rocky ground, and when it came up, the plants withered because they had no moisture. Other seed fell among thorns, which grew up with it and choked the plants. Still other seed fell on good soil. It came up and yielded a crop, a hundred times more than was sown." When He said this, He called out, "Whoever has ears to hear, let them hear."

His disciples asked him what this parable meant. He said, "The knowledge of the secrets of the kingdom of God has been given to you, but to others I speak in parables, so that, 'though seeing, they may not see; though hearing, they may not understand.'

"This is the meaning of the parable: The seed is the word of God. Those along the path are the ones who hear, and then the devil comes and takes away the word from their hearts, so that they may not believe and be saved. Those

on the rocky ground are the ones who receive the word with joy when they hear it, but they have no root. They believe for a while, but in the time of testing they fall away. The seed that fell among thorns stands for those who hear, but as they go on their way they are choked by life's worries, riches and pleasures, and they do not mature. But the seed on good soil stands for those with a noble and good heart, who hear the word, retain it, and by persevering produce a crop" (Luke 8:4–15).

Listening to the Story

I wonder if Jesus was an introvert. When the crowds were the largest is when Jesus spoke some of his hardest truths, almost as if to scare people off. Let's face it, Jesus said some ornery things:

Let the dead bury their own dead (Matt. 8:21).

Gouge it [your eye] *out and throw it away* (Matt. 5:29).

Sell everything you have (Mark 10:21).

Eat my flesh and drink my blood (John 6:56 NRSV).

Hate [your] *father and mother* (Luke 14:26).

On these occasions, Jesus metaphorically taught that following Him would not necessarily be easy. Jesus desires dedication. How would you have felt hearing Jesus speak this way? Sadly, I am not sure how long I would have stuck around. Jesus directly addresses the cost of following Him in His "It'll cost you" parable (see chapter 14, beginning on page 116).

Here, Jesus is inundated with an exceptionally large crowd of people, yet this time Jesus does not speak harsh words. In fact, Jesus tells one of his easier-to-understand stories to let His followers know just how to effectively listen, embrace His message, and live it out. Jesus even explains the parable for us. Some of the parables are odd and tricky to understand, head-scratchers for sure. In this case, we have the benefit of Jesus wonderfully explaining it.

The Explanation. The seed stands for the words of God. The various soils stand for people who either embrace His words, are moderately or initially open, or those who run for the exits. Some will accept His words as a child says yes to ice cream. Others dabble for a while but later go their own way.

In Matthew's version of this parable, Jesus quotes Isaiah 6:9 to help explain why.

You will listen and listen but won't understand. You will look and look but not see. This people's heart has gone flabby and fat (translation by N. T. Wright).[1]

This story of a farmer and various soils enlightens us as to how we too can have a flabby heart if we are not careful. It shows how Jesus and His words can slip by us without us even noticing. It all comes down to the receptivity of our hearts.

When Jesus compared hearts to soil, this would have come alive for first-century Galileans. Why? They were country folk who toiled in the dirt. They knew very well how hard it was to get good soil. Much of the hill country of Galilee is hard limestone, and getting good soil takes work.[2] It takes patient endurance of working the soil over countless years. Jesus describes soil—and hearts—as either *hard, rocky, thorny,* or *fertile*.

A *fertile* heart is one that is eager and accepting. It describes a person who is excited to hear from Jesus. But hearing from God takes more than excitement alone, it takes patience. Let's be honest. It takes being intentional and patient to sit with God long enough to hear Him speak to our hearts. And it takes patient endurance (*hypomone*) to see His character develop in our own life. But the toil is worth it. Spiritual growth takes time.

Jesus also explains each less effective soil (heart) type. First, we can simply ignore Him (*hard soil*). Our life can be too full of noise, and we can be too busy to notice God speaking to us. In our hectic lives, it can be a struggle to quiet our thoughts enough to hear God speak. And it takes more than being quiet. It takes being present.

The Lord is good to those who wait for him, to the soul who seeks him. It is good that one should wait quietly (Lam. 3:25-26 ESV).

Or, we can eagerly accept His words, yet when trouble (*rocky soil*) comes, we doubt the love of God. The temperature in Palestine can be extremely hot, so young plants can quickly die after sprouting due to lack of water and shallow roots.[3] When knocked down by hardship, it is possible to become bitter, never forgiving God for the pain we may experience in our life.

Finally, we can be too consumed by our interests or possessions (*thorny soil)* that compete for our attention. Like weeds, anything less than God can choke out our love for Him.[4] Weeds do not overgrow all at once. Yet, once those weeds grow into mature plants, they are tough to get rid of. Oh, how we love our toys, don't we? And we certainly crave our next fun-filled adventure! There are so many ways to be entertained in our world today.

The Message. This parable is most often used for salvation. Granted, it is that, but we don't have to stop there! I believe Jesus also uses the soil metaphor to explain that He desires to do a bit of cultivating in our hearts. It's a matter of how receptive we will be to this transformational work.

How do we allow God to cultivate our hearts? I believe our soul is nurtured as we spend quality time with God, in His Word, and in quieting our minds enough to listen for His love. It is being present in His presence.

Let the morning bring me word of your unfailing love, for I have put my trust in you (Psalm 143:8).

Behold, I will allure her, and bring her into the wilderness and speak tenderly to her (Hosea 2:14).

How fertile is the soil of your heart? Do you make space for God? Do you intentionally listen and allow God to dig up your hard and brittle parts? Have you been overly consumed with pleasure or attaining—at the expense of enjoying God?

Just as having a lean body takes effort to work off the flab, do you make the effort to root out your crud? Ask God where to start. Ask God to show you how you can have a fertile heart. And it is well worth your time to seek out help from a spiritual director or counselor.

The journey to happiness involves finding the courage to go down into yourself and take responsibility for what's there: all of it. —Richard Rohr

Intimacy with Jesus is all about our heart's receptivity. Do you allow for daily spaces to simply be with God? Do you truly listen for His still, small voice of love throughout your day?

The Sower. Finally, the power of this parable doesn't end with our heart's receptivity. We simply must notice that it is God doing the seed sowing! It is not up to us alone. He speaks words of love, to whoever will listen. After telling his story, Jesus then belts out:

Whoever has ears to hear, let them hear! (Luke 8:8)

I think this was the you-could-hear-a-pin-drop moment! Jesus wants us to know that God is going to speak! The only question is, will we listen? Will we slow down enough to hear?

What may not be apparent at first glance is that to the original crowd, the farmer in the story may have seemed a little off his rocker. Let me explain. The farmer seemingly wasted so many seeds! He threw seeds everywhere! A good farmer surely would not bother throwing seeds where they would not take root. They might have cringed at the farmer's waste.

We should not so much cringe but jump in excitement! God's infinite love for us should never cease to amaze us. Like the careless farmer throwing seeds, God tosses His love everywhere and to everyone! God is always leaning in, whispering to us—we only need to listen. God always desires your company, wherever you are, and whatever the circumstances. God never gives up on you. Let's take a quick inventory of how God's extravagant love is portrayed in the parables.

- God is like a happy-go-lucky farmer who indiscriminately throws seed wherever it lands, just in case it takes root. (Luke 8:4–15)

- God is like an extravagant landowner, who keeps going into the marketplace to get more and more workers—despite the unfairness to those who have worked all day for the same wage. He can't help but go back for more. (Matthew 20:1–16)

- God is like an over-the-top party-giver who so desperately wants a special feast for his child that He grabs anybody willing to join the fun before they can say no. (Luke 14:16–24)

- God is like a risk-taking shepherd who leaves his entire herd to rescue the one who is lost, afraid, and in danger. (Luke 15:3–7)

- God is like a beside-himself father who runs out into the street, shedding any remnant of respectability to embrace his long lost, pig-smelling, betrayer son.[5] (Luke 15:11–24)

We cannot miss this truth! God will always chase us down! He will search us out, find us, embrace us, and love us like we are his very own. Why? Because that is who we are. We are loved without limit by a God who has none!

And so, in the big picture, it's not about us at all, is it? He desires to be with all of us! He loves every single one of us.

I suppose Jesus is not an introvert after all. He wants us all to enjoy Him forever!

Entering the Story

As a farmer, I have a simple motto—when you plant a seed, you believe in tomorrow. Believing my seeds will grow into fruitful plants is what I do. My family has farmed in Galilee for generations. Our farm is small, but our soil is especially fertile.

Having a great harvest starts with the soil. Our fertile land did not come easy. It was originally full of rocks we dug out over generations. And it is hard work. Every time I plow, I manage to find a few rocks that need to be removed.

This morning Mary, Joanna, and Susanna stopped by my farm to buy produce. It seems they are helping feed and manage the affairs of the Rabbi Jesus and His followers. They appeared pleased with my vegetables. That felt good. They also invited me to come hear Him teach. I think I will.

On my way to hear Jesus, I noticed that His followers trampled on some of my crops. *Stay on the pathway people,* I thought to myself! *You just ruined all my hard work.*

Jesus began to teach, and I felt immediately drawn to Him. Why wouldn't I, for He told a farming story! How cool is that? He told of a farmer sowing seeds and how the ones that landed on the best soil produced a great crop as compared to the ones that fell on a hard pathway. I cynically wondered, *Is Jesus referring to my trampled crops?* I guess I was still a little angry.

As Jesus described the rich, fertile soil, He reached down and grabbed a handful of my soil. My heart jumped. He called my soil great! One of His disciples looked my way and winked.

Jesus then said, "The seed represents the Word of God, who stands before you now. The rich soil symbolizes a good and tender heart who lets me in. Having good soil is having a heart to listen. Good soil is the heart who loves what I love."

Jesus looked right at me and continued, "From a fertile, receptive heart, good things will grow—love, peace, gentleness, kindness, and grace. Special things will grow, just like the wonderful vegetables you have grown." I felt ten feet tall! I could not believe Jesus honored me like that! I almost forgot about my trampled plants.

After Jesus' story, everyone was enjoying the sunny afternoon. It felt good to take a break from my hard work and visit with such kind people. Then, I nearly jumped out of my skin when Jesus walked up and asked to speak to me!

Jesus asked, "How did you like my story?"

I told Him, "Very much so."

Jesus said, "There is more to the story that I want you to hear. The soil represents your heart. And just like it is hard work to develop fertile soil, it takes work to be a loving person. There may be rocks to remove. You harbor hurts and bitterness, don't you? We need to dig those up. Will you let Me help? Let's do it together."

At these words, tears began to flow. His words deeply touched my emotions in a way I was not expecting. The way Jesus took the time to lovingly speak to me was beyond wonderful. I deeply fell in love with Jesus that afternoon.

Jesus sees a world of potential in me. Jesus believes in a wonderful tomorrow for me!

Living the Story

In depicting different soils, Jesus was not simply referring to individuals and their relative openness to Jesus' words. He was also referring to parts within each of us that are either open or closed.[6]

• Where are you most

Point of the Parable:

God generously spreads seeds of love into the soil of our hearts. We only need to receive.

God continually knocks on the door of our hearts with extravagant love.

Jesus said, "Have a heart open to love."

God never has and never will give up on us. For we are loved without limit by a God who has none.

open to God? When and where do you hear Him best? When do you most feel His presence? How are you touched by His love? This is your good soil. Relish your good soil and crave more of it.

- What is your rocky soil? Perhaps you are more loving at home but less so at work. Or, maybe for you, it is the other way around. In what environment do you tend to hold onto grudges? What part of your life is too full of weeds? Are you simply too busy to hear God? What rocks does God want to dislodge from your life? Allow plenty of time to listen for God to speak to you.

A Blessing for You, on Your Journey of Listening

May God's over-the-top, extravagant love flood your heart. No matter what you have done or how you feel, may you allow yourself to be loved by Love Himself.

May you rejoice that God is tenderly at work to nurture love and compassion in you. May you simply say yes to His presence today.

May you even allow God the painful task of pulling whatever weeds need plucking out of your life. And may you stop noticing the weeds in those around you.

May you feel God's embrace. May you know, really know, that you are infinitely loved, without any limits by a God who has none.

7

Good Bad Guy

To be truly good means being a good neighbor. And to be a good neighbor means recognizing that there are ultimately no strangers. Everybody is my neighbor! —Brian D. McLaren[1]

On one occasion an expert in the law stood up to test Jesus. "Teacher," he asked, "what must I do to inherit eternal life?" "What is written in the Law?" Jesus replied. "How do you read it?" He answered, "Love the Lord your God with all your heart and with all your soul and with all your strength and with all your mind; and love your neighbor as yourself." "You have answered correctly," Jesus replied. "Do this and you will live."

But he wanted to justify himself, so he asked Jesus, "And who is my neighbor?"

In reply, Jesus said: "A man was going down from Jerusalem to Jericho, when he was attacked by robbers. They stripped him of his clothes, beat him and went away, leaving him half dead. A priest happened to be going down the same road, and when he saw the man, he passed by on the other side. So too, a Levite, when he came to the place and saw him, passed by on the other side. But a Samaritan, as he traveled, came where the man was; and when he saw him, he took pity on him. He

*went to him and bandaged his wounds, pouring on oil
and wine. Then he put the man on his own donkey,
brought him to an inn and took care of him. The next day
he took out two denarii and gave them to the innkeeper.
'Look after him,' he said, 'and when I return, I will reim-
burse you for any extra expense you may have.' Which of
these three do you think was a neighbor to the man who
fell into the hands of robbers?"*

*The expert in the law replied, "The one who had mercy
on him." Jesus told him, "Go and do likewise"* (Luke
10:25–37).

Listening to the Story

How do I get into heaven? How can, I be sure? Have you ever
wondered that? Jesus was asked that by an expert in the law and
this forms the setting for our parable.

We must notice a couple of things about the expert's question.
First, it wasn't really an honest one. His motive was more about
making himself look good and to put Jesus on the spot. As a result,
Jesus answers him with a few questions of his own, "What is
written in the law? How do you read it?"

Secondly, the word "do" (*poiesas*) in "What must I do," was in
a tense that suggests a single, limited action, as if it were something to check off a to-do list. The expert was thinking in terms of
a single action, a one-off, rather than a lifelong journey of growing
in love. He thought eternal life was something to earn, rather than
something that God freely gives.[2]

The answer to the expert's question was an easy one. Hebrew
children memorized the very verses (Deut. 6:5, Lev. 19:18) needed
to solve this important riddle. In addition, at times men literally

wore a copy of these verses written on parchment and placed in small leather boxes—one around their wrist and the other on their forehead.[3] It shouldn't be too hard coming up with the answer when you are wearing it! Maybe the expert even had his phylactery (what the leather boxes are called) on at the time!

So, the expert did what any expert should be able to do. He proudly answered, "Love the Lord your God with all your heart, soul, strength, and mind; and love your neighbor as yourself." The fact that we should love God above all else is repeated over and over in the Torah (Deut. 6:5, 10:12, 11:13, 19:9, 30:6, etc.). To love God above all else was a Hebrew's primary objective in life and the expert knew this well.

We also need to clearly understand this truth for ourselves. How do we get into heaven? Love. How do we please God? Love. We need to know the importance love should play in our lives. It should be our heartbeat, our calling card, our primary goal, and our endgame. Above anything and everything, we should love. Please take time to contemplate this.

We are to love God with every ounce of strength we have. But let's be honest—that's hard to do! The expert knew this as well. and so he thought he would change the focus a little. He asked, "Who is my neighbor?" Nice try, I suppose.

If we are perfectly honest, we struggle with this same question. Just who are we obligated to love? There are so many people in the world, surely, I cannot love them all! So, Jesus, would it be good enough if I love a more manageable number? How about if I concentrate on loving the people that I like? That's hard enough at times. It seems a little more achievable if I could at least try and love "my people" well! Loving everyone is frankly just too hard!

So, in response to the expert, and to us, Jesus tells a story. Don't you love that? In order to have any chance at deciphering the story's message, we first must understand a few things about the culture of their day.

The Samaritan. In Jesus' day, Jews and Samaritans hated each other, plain and simple. It went back to centuries of disagreement and wars and resulted in a deep-rooted bigotry and resentment. Samaritans were a racial mix of Assyrian and Hebrew. So, they were a mix of ethnicity and were considered impure in the eyes of the Jews.

Since the Jews did not accept them, nor allow them to worship in the temple in Jerusalem, the Samaritans built their own temple in 388 BCE. They needed a place to worship, after all. It was destroyed in 128 BCE by the Jewish King Hyrcanus. That didn't help the relationship to say the least. It was rebuilt again by Herod the Great.[4] Samaritans worshipped in their own way and in their own temple.

I once naively asked a dear friend, who happens to be African American, "What do you think, would you prefer to worship in a mostly black church or in a church with a broad diversity of color?" His answer hit hard. "Sam, the only reason there are black churches is because we weren't welcome in white churches." The truth stung.

Yes, the hatred between Jews and Samaritans in Jesus' day ran deep. Once, Jesus was slandered as a "Samaritan and demon-possessed" to his face (John 8:48). I am not sure which part was meant to be worse! The words were clearly intended to ridicule and demean Jesus.

The bottom line is that Hebrews looked at Samaritans as an inferior race with an inferior religion. Interesting. I am glad today we never have a problem loving people from a different race or religion—pun very much intended! We often have a hard time with someone who just makes a better casserole than ours, nonetheless with someone who burned down our church!

The Road to Jericho. The second thing we must understand is what the road from Jerusalem to Jericho was like. Jerusalem sits at an elevation of around 2500 feet above sea level, while Jericho is at 800 feet below sea level. That is an elevation gain of 3300 feet in seventeen miles. On foot, that's a healthy hike! The road was a treacherous stretch of dirt. It was not only steep, but it was a winding pathway through desolate desert famous for bandits. In the fifth century, Jerome called it the "Red or Bloody Way."[5]

Often bandits would fake an injury to get a passerby to stop. Only a fool would travel this highway alone and perhaps Jesus' audience would have viewed our traveler in the parable as such. Jericho was a popular residence for priests. Each order of priests served in the Temple for one week (Luke 1:8) and would travel this exact road.[6] Jesus used an actual place and typical events for his imaginative story.

It is important to remember, even though this parable may be familiar to us, the original audience would have very much expected the priest and the Levite to help the poor guy left for dead in the ditch, even if it were risky. The punch of the parable is that the two respected religious leaders in the story do not stop and help. And the ultimate shock was that a hated Samaritan does! This is incredibly significant on two levels.

The hated character in Jesus' story, who the listeners may have thought was responsible for beating up the traveler in the first place, turns out to be the person who loved.

Jesus did not tell a story of who to love (remember, this is the original question), His story depicted a hated enemy as *having* great love! Jesus completely flipped their expectations. Jesus has a way of turning our thinking upside down!

The Message. The point of this parable is clearly that there should be no limit to who we love. Yet, I believe it goes even deeper, much deeper. Why? Jesus made the villain loveable. Jesus made the person that is so hard for us to love, the one who loves us! It's kind of painful when someone we don't like happens to be a wonderfully likeable person to everyone else, isn't it?

Jesus depicted our devil as an angel! This flips the message on its head. Jesus is saying to love well is to see our enemy as a lovely person. When Jesus made the Samaritan the one who exhibited God's love, Jesus had our worst enemy portray God! Now, that's a story that packs a punch.

The ones who disappoint you, need you the most.
—Jack Hyles

Mother Teresa was able to love and help the poorest, most desperate people, those who would make you and I turn our heads because she "saw Jesus in everyone." These are her words, not mine. Thomas Merton put it this way: "Our job is to love others without stopping to inquire whether or not they are worthy."

It's in our nature to put people into boxes in our minds. We mentally put people into likeable or unlikeable categories. We label people as either interesting or boring, as someone to look up to or someone beneath us. I sadly admit—I am guilty as charged. How about you? Have you ever considered that when we do it, we're putting Jesus into our unlikeable box? Ouch.

Every time we draw a line between us and others,
Jesus is always on the other side of it.
—Nadia Bolz-Weber

The power of this good-bad-guy story is that there really is not a bad guy. It turns out that the one whom we thought was good, wasn't that great after all. And our personal villain was the hero!

Everyone is created by the same God. And this same God loves us all the same. Everyone has the potential for good. A Christian should be brave enough to see the good in others—even in those we would rather hate. If we could only learn to strip away our preconceived judgments and see others anew for who they really are.

How do we get into heaven? For starters, there is no reason why heaven cannot start in the here and now. For heaven is where

God is, and God is right here if we only look for Him. How do we get into heaven? Love! Love God. Love others. It's that simple. No need for an expert. Anyone can do it.

Entering the Story

I know the great summary of my faith—to love my God with all my heart and with all my soul and with all my strength and mind! I know I should love God with my deepest passions, with the very core of who I am, and to love Him with every thought. That is a tall order, but that's the goal.

I also know I am to love others as much as I love myself. I am to care for others' physical and emotional needs like I care for my own. That seems like an even loftier goal. I cannot catch a break it seems! I know what I am asked to do, but how can I genuinely do it?

As I was sitting with this parable and pondering this, Jesus told me a story. Jesus gave me a good-bad-guy story of my own.

I imagined I was on a run on a gorgeous mountain trail. I love trail running. I feel such joy trekking through large stretches of beautiful country. I love feeling the wind at my back and my strong legs carrying me up and over mountain passes. I cherish feeling God's presence in His creation.

But on this run, it was not only joy I felt. Suddenly, my toe caught a rock and down I went down hard. I trashed my ankle and felt blood ease out of an elbow and knee. I had run a long way and was physically spent. And now I was hurt. I was alone and unable to get myself back to the trailhead. I was in trouble!

My favorite singer/songwriter (Jon Foreman) came running up with a ukulele strung over his shoulder. He played me a quick tune but then ran off. "Sorry, I'm late for a gig." I love Jon's heart and his music. Oh well.

One of my favorite pastors (Nadia Bolz-Weber) ran up and shouted, "Damn, you're hurt bad, dude! Wish I could help, but you're not my people!" I love her fresh take on our faith. Oh well.

Finally, my favorite elite trail runner (Courtney Dauwalter) was now in sight. She's one of the most gifted trail runners on the planet. And yet she always encourages others on the trail. Surely, she will help! With glistening form, she glides past me at a record pace. She had a race to win. Oh well.

Finally, just before dark, when all hope seemed lost, a rather obese guy comes waddling up, covered in lousy tattoos all over his chest, neck, and arms. His sweaty gut was protruding out from under a camo shirt, conveniently hanging over his shorts. His words were hard to understand. His constant slobbering from the wad of chew in his mouth didn't help. His teeth were stained a nasty black, and he smelled of sweat and cheap cologne.

He blurted out, "Sir, are you okay?" Now, I was hoping this guy would keep going! I flat out did not want this character's help. No such luck. He says, "Buddy, I'm gonna get you outta here," as he hoists me up with his brawny arms. With every step, I could smell his chew and taste the drench of his sweat. You see, my face was resting on his big belly.

This dude was nasty, but this guy is just who I need. This loveable, tender bear-of-a-man with the strength of an ox and the kindness of Mother Theresa flat out saved my life. He cared for me like a brother.

I then heard Jesus say, "Sam, who should you love? Who is your neighbor?"

Who does God ask us to love? Anyone we meet on our "trail," that's who! Anyone who needs our help. And we should especially take notice when the people that we don't even like end up being our heroes. It's time to listen and learn when those we hate are the very ones doing the loving!

How do we love others as we should? By seeing God's goodness in others, that's how! It's our only chance. The goodness in them may be buried and deep, but by loving them we can help draw it out. And often, our bad guys are really the loveable ones if we only take the time to notice.

(Please note, the above-mentioned people I greatly admire and are used for imaginative and illustrative purposes only. I am sure in real life, each of them would go out of their way to help someone!)

Living the Story

Sit with the following story and ponder how you can love the unlovable in your life.

A father and a son boarded a train for a journey home. The son was 24 years old, yet was acting like a child, to the dismay of others on the train. The boy could not contain himself. He had his head out the window and was blurting out with a loud voice for all to hear.

"Dad, look, the trees are going behind us! Look at the trees!" His dad smiled. "Dad, look, the clouds are running with us! Look at the clouds!" There was no end to his excitement.

A young couple sitting nearby, rather annoyed at the boy's childish behavior, couldn't take it any longer and said to the father, "Can you get your son to behave himself? Can't he just sit quietly? Why don't you take your son to see a doctor and find out what's wrong with him?"

The father smiled and said, "I did, and we are just coming from the hospital. My son was blind from birth, and he just got his eyesight today. And he can look out the window all he damn well pleases!"

This is a great lesson

Point of the Parable:

The only way to genuinely love others is to see them as lovely.

How do we please God? It starts with recognizing the beauty in everyone.

Jesus said, "Even your worst enemy knows how to love. Do the same."

There should be absolutely no limit to our love.

---

in not criticizing others before we know their story. This is a lesson in seeing the joy and beauty in everyone.

It's as though *our* lives should shout out loud for all to hear, "Father, I see you! Look at this lovely person! I see you everywhere I look!" And those around us may think that we need a doctor! But no. Our heavenly Father will say with delight, "There is no need for a doctor, he simply has My eyes. He sees the good in everyone, just like I do. He sees the potential in everyone. He sees what I see!"

Work on changing your awareness. See Jesus in others. Notice others as who they are—crafted by God as beautiful and good. They may need a little help in healing a few wounds and in seeing the good in themselves.

A Blessing for You, on Your journey into Love

May God's love appear in unexpected ways—perhaps in a wonderful act from a friend or a foe. May God's love penetrate your heart so that you see the good in the person who has rubbed you wrong.

May God comfort the parts of you that feel battered and left for dead. May God ease your pain, allow you to stop worrying, and grant you a peace you cannot explain.

May you find joy in building others up. May you resist the effort to position yourself; instead, may you applaud others and allow them to get the credit, even when it should have gone to you.

May you feel loved by God all through this day. May you know that God feels you are loveable!

8

Friend in Need

Some are sad. And some are glad. And some are very, very bad. Why are they sad and glad and bad? I do not know. Go ask your dad. —Dr. Seuss

Then Jesus said to them, "Suppose you have a friend, and you go to him at midnight and say, 'Friend, lend me three loaves of bread; a friend of mine on a journey has come to me, and I have no food to offer him.' And suppose the one inside answers, 'Don't bother me. The door is already locked, and my children and I are in bed. I can't get up and give you anything.' I tell you, even though he will not get up and give you the bread because of friendship, yet because of your shameless audacity he will surely get up and give you as much as you need.

"So, I say to you: 'Ask and it will be given to you; seek and you will find; knock and the door will be opened to you. For everyone who asks receives; the one who seeks finds; and to the one who knocks, the door will be opened.

'Which of you fathers, if your son asks for a fish, will give him a snake instead? Or if he asks for an egg, will give him a scorpion? If you then, though you are evil, know how to give good gifts to your children, how much

more will your Father in heaven give the Holy Spirit to those who ask him!'" (Luke 11:5–13).

Listening to the Story

Can you teach me to pray? What a sweet question.

I asked a Jesuit spiritual director that once, and he giggled with delight. He literally giggled. Over the next few days, he taught me many wonderful ways to pray. Most of them I still use. I would be missing out if I had never asked.

The disciples asked, "Lord, teach us to pray" (Luke 11:1). I wonder if Jesus giggled. They asked after watching Jesus do what He did best—pray. Maybe you have felt that way when you have been with a person who genuinely loves to pray. You may deeply desire to grow in prayer. You may avoid praying at all costs! Or perhaps, you are in between—you would love to pray more but never seem to have the time or energy. Praying can feel like work. Have you ever considered asking Jesus like the disciples did?

There is something very tender and heartwarming about the disciple's request. I am sure it was meaningful for Jesus, so much so, He taught them the "Lord's Prayer," and then told them a story immediately after. Jesus taught them *what* to pray and then *how* to pray. Our parable is the how.

Jesus' story poses a scenario, starting with the question, "*Suppose you...?*" Do you see what Jesus is doing here? Jesus is inviting us to put ourselves into His story.

Suppose you have a friend who shows up at your door in the middle of the night, weary and hungry from a long journey. You are not prepared to honor your friend and his family with a meal. Realizing you are in a pickle; you seek out the help of your neighbor and friend. You knock on his door and ask for help. You cry out, "Do you have any food? Anything? Just some bread perhaps? I am desperate. Can you please help me out?" Jesus asks us to imagine being in that pickle and seeking, knocking, and asking for help.

The implied question is, could you ever see this happening and your neighbor not giving you some bread? The obvious answer is no! This would never happen! A good friend or neighbor would gladly give you whatever they had, no matter how late it was. It may take a bit of knocking to wake them up, but help they would. It was especially so in first-century Palestine.

Pick the neighbor, before the house. —Arab Proverb

The Culture. Hospitality in the ancient world was of paramount importance. Most travelers relied on the hospitality of friends, and the host had a responsibility to care for his guest. Inns were few, and it's not like they had a nearby drive-through to grab a meal in a pinch. Baking was done outside in an open courtyard, took considerable time, and involved more than one person. A neighbor would easily know who had baked bread that day (Jeremiah 7:18).[1]

Also, in ancient Palestine, life was very public. In the morning, doors were open, and anyone might wander in and out. We saw this for ourselves living in the Middle East. People would freely come into our house. Let me tell you, it took a little getting used to! One time, my wife had a strange man follow her into our bedroom to innocently ask her a question. She turned around and got quite a surprise! He wondered why she was so upset.

However, in first-century life, when a door was shut and barred for the night, it was different. It meant you did not want to be disturbed. No one would invade that privacy![2] Jesus' audience would have understood that knocking on a locked door at night meant desperation.

The Message. The story teaches us a lot about prayer. For starters, we should pray even when it does not make sense, and we feel there is little hope. Even when we are desperate, and it seems like all the doors are barred shut, we should pray. God will answer, even more so than a reluctant neighbor awakened from his sleep. Let's look at a few of the ways this story teaches us how to pray.

Pray Shamelessly. In Luke 11:8, Jesus says, "Because of your shameless audacity he will surely get up and give you as much as you need." The Greek word (*anaideia*) is used only here in all of scripture and refers to having no sense of shame; to willingly engage in improper conduct.

The parable encourages us to pray boldly. Yet, it is not suggesting we should be demanding, rude, or weird with God. This is more of a parable of contrast, a how-much-more-than story. The meaning is, if a request was granted even when the character in the story was desperately discourteous, how much more will your loving Father respond to your humble requests.[3]

There is no perfect way to pray. God does not mind how we come to Him; He simply wants us to come. We tend to go it alone way too often, out of our over-inflated egos. And it goes against our grain to admit to God that we need help. We may resist asking God for His mercy yet again for the umpteenth time regarding the same issue. God does not mind. We need to realize God is more eager to give than we are to ask. So, pray shamelessly.

Pray Openly. Pray without an agenda. Jesus concluded by saying, "If you then, who are evil, know how to give good gifts to your children, how much more will your heavenly Father give the Holy Spirit to those who ask him." This is a reminder that God is all about giving us good things. He may not necessarily provide exactly what we *ask for*, but God will give us what we *need*. And often the best thing He can give us is simply His presence.

As we previously mentioned, Jesus taught His disciples *what to pray* with the Lord's prayer. He followed that with a story illustrating *how to pray* (shamelessly and openly). Jesus then concludes with *why pray*.

Ask, Seek, and Knock. Jesus says to ask, seek, and knock, and it will be given! Why should we bother praying? Because God will answer, that is why! And unlike the neighbor in the story, God's door is always open. He never sleeps! (Psalm 121:4) When we ask, seek, and knock, God is there. God openly, lovingly, and graciously gives!

And God is forever available to always give you the best gift ever, Himself.

God, help me to shamelessly ask You for what I need. Father, help me to passionately seek You and Your presence. Help me to realize You are always with me.

God, thank You that You always care. You always forgive. You always give!

Jesus, teach me to pray. I want to enjoy Your giggle.

Entering the Story

I am chuckling now just thinking about it! Not long ago I experienced being the neighbor that did not want to get out of bed. That's right.

My wife and I were vacationing in a gorgeous coastal area of California. Our room was more like a cozy little cabin than a hotel room. From our balcony, we could see the ocean and hear the waves crash against the chiseled rocks. We live in the mountains, and as beautiful as they are, the ocean is a refreshing change of scenery and wonderful getaway.

Our room had its own fireplace, which was the sole source of heat. Each night, I would build a fire for warmth but also to add the dancing of light on the walls and the crackling of the fire. The atmosphere was almost magical.

One night I deadbolted the door which, to me at least, meant we were not to be disturbed. We settled into bed enjoying the fire and ocean waves and drifted off to sleep with a peace that is hard to describe. Suddenly, our peaceful slumber was rudely interrupted! Someone was knocking at the door. My half-awake mind did not even want to try and decipher who it might be.

Answering the door would mean ditching my nice warm covers and walking the unsurmountable ten steps to the door. So, I called out from bed, "Please go away. We are fine!" *She must not have heard me,* I thought, for she kept knocking, only a little louder.

So, what do I do? I yell a little louder, "No, thanks. Please go away!" What does she do? She knocks louder still, so I yell back, a little louder still. The louder I yelled, the louder she knocked! She was determined!

My wife finally said, "Honey, stop your crazy yelling and answer the door!" Her words exuded a mountain-sized amount of frustration over her silly husband. Begrudgingly, I went to the door and said, "Thank you, but we don't need our bed turned over. Oh, but yes, we will take those extra towels." I always take extra towels!

One could sense the satisfaction in all the cabins within earshot of my yelling!

I got back in bed, and my wife and I laughed for several minutes at my madness. Here, I had just lived out the parable I had been reading! The timing could not have been better orchestrated.

As I remember my absurdity and ponder Jesus' story, the meaning of the parable is clear. God will never be as silly as me! God will never close and deadbolt His door. The door to His presence is always open wide! And I am free to walk in.

When I ask, He is always there to answer. When I seek, He always allows Himself to be found. And when I knock, He always, always, always answers.

Thank You, Father God, that Your love is infinitely bigger than mine, that You are infinitely more caring and compassionate than me, even at my best. Thank You that You are ever present. That you always hear, always listen, and always answer. These truths make me chuckle with delight.

Living the Story

Was there a time you either lived out the shameless neighbor in need or perhaps the neighbor with his door barred hoping the person outside would go away? Have fun remembering that event. Can you relate it to the parable? Also, ponder the following exercises.

- Recall a time when you shamelessly went to God for something you desperately needed. How did God answer your prayer? Was it just what you asked for? If not, and if you felt betrayed by God, go to Him now and let Him know how you felt. Ask Him to show you why He did not give you what you so desperately needed.

- Let's turn Dr. Seuss' riddle into a prayer: Am I sad? Am I glad? Am I bad? I am asking you, Dad.

God, I am asking you to identify my emotions today. What are they and why am I feeling this way? Are they an insight into a hurt that needs healed? Do I feel pure joy that needs to be explored?

> Point of the Parable:
>
> **God is eager to give. We simply ask. God is easily found when we look.**
>
> "Can you teach us to pray?" they asked.
>
> Jesus said, "See God as your friend who is always eager to help."
>
> All we need to do is ask.

- This week, in your daily prayers, ask God for simply His presence. Ask God to be with you in tangible ways. Then notice Him show up in ways you never thought possible. Journal your times with Him.

A Blessing for You, the Seeker

May God's door of love feel wide open for you. May you feel welcome in His presence. May you know you are an honored guest.

May you be brave enough to keep knocking, even when He is quiet. May you find joy in the seeking, in the knocking, and in the asking—in simply being with Him.

May God's presence invade your space so much so that you feel a warmth like sitting near a fire and a peace like listening to gentle ocean waves break against the shore.

May you hear God's giggle of delight as you turn to Him with an open heart. May your prayer be, "God teach me. I am here."

9

Hitting It Big

We suffer to get well. We surrender to win. We die to live. We give it away to keep it. —*Fr. Richard Rohr*

Someone out of the crowd said, "Teacher, order my brother to give me a fair share of the family inheritance." He replied, "Mister, what makes you think it's any of my business to be a judge or mediator for you?" Speaking to the people, He went on, "Take care! Protect yourself against the least bit of greed. Life is not defined by what you have, even when you have a lot."

Then He told them this story: "The farm of a certain rich man produced a terrific crop. He talked to himself: 'What can I do? My barn isn't big enough for this harvest.' Then He said, 'Here's what I'll do: I'll tear down my barns and build bigger ones. Then I'll gather in all my grain and goods, and I'll say to myself, Self, you've done well! You've got it made and can now retire. Take it easy and have the time of your life!'

"Just then God showed up and said, 'Fool! Tonight, you die. And your barnful of goods—who gets it?' That's what happens when you fill your barn with Self and not with God" (Luke 12:13–21 The Message).

Listening to the Story

Ouch. As I pen my thoughts on this parable, the stock market is in its fourth week of crashing. It is falling and falling fast. Our country is in the early stages of the 2020 pandemic, and folks are panicking. Panic buyers are hoarding toilet paper, and panic sellers are attempting to cut losses on Wall Street. It's a sad but understandable juxtaposition of fear for one's health and protecting valuable assets. All because of a nasty parasite we cannot even see.

Jesus remarkably used stories to teach about money matters. If we are honest with ourselves and this story, it may strike a painful nerve. It may hurt a little. But only if we admit we can relate to the farmer. You see, at first glance, the guy who hit it big seems to have done a perfectly reasonable thing. Isn't the dream for a lot of us to make enough to retire early? We may be wondering, what is the harm in that?

Our character in the story built extra barns to protect his assets. He too was guilty of hoarding, not of toilet paper, but of his rich harvest. This parable may cause us to reconsider our view of what "making it" should look like.

And here I am, I have personally built a barn, and I am retired. Ouch! I guess it is true, this parable hits close to home!

Let's be honest. We value success. We strive for financial security. I believe the warning given in the parable is not so much in having success or possessions, but in how tightly we cling to them. Yet, we are not doing the parable justice if we do not honestly take stock in how we personally value money.[1]

The Culture. Before we go too far, we need to understand some first-century context. Jesus was asked to settle a dispute between brothers over an inheritance. Since civil disputes were often over how to interpret the Hebrew Scriptures, rabbis and teachers were often asked to intervene. Inheritance laws instruct that the oldest brother was to receive double what the other brothers received (Deut. 21:15–17). Apparently, the younger brother felt he did not get his fair share.[2]

Besides giving guidance on inheritance issues, the Hebrew Scriptures say a lot about guarding against trusting wealth instead of God, such as:

If I have made gold my trust...I would have been false to God above (Job 31:24, 28 ESV).

Let not the rich man boast in his riches (Jer. 9:23 ESV).

Honor the Lord with your wealth (Prov. 3:9).

So, this story should have only strengthened what they already knew—to not overvalue money. But, to me, the punch line of the story, the part Jesus wanted to drive home is found at the very end of the parable. It is the core of why Jesus told it. The problem is not big barns. The problem is if our barns are only filled with self!

That's what happens when you fill your barn with self and not with God (Luke 12:21, The Message).

Jesus is not so much addressing an over-stuffed barn but an over-inflated ego! What is our ego anyway? Interesting enough, ego originated from both the Greek and Latin word for "I." Simple as that.

Our ego refers to our self-esteem or self-image. Having a positive one is great and necessary. Having an over-inflated one is not! The farmer in the parable had quite an unhealthy ego. He was entirely too self-focused and self-absorbed. Let's see how.

Self-focused. You would probably be hard pressed to find another story this short with so many "I's" and "my's" in it. The farmer really was not harvesting grain but his own ego! He had a rather funny conversation with himself. "What can I do? My barn isn't big enough for my harvest. I know what I'll do. I'll tear down my barns and build myself bigger ones! Then I'll gather in all my grain." Notice all the I's? It's ridiculous.

The farmer in this story never sees beyond himself. The focus of his world is himself. Someone once described a girl named Edith, who was a bit self-focused, "Edith lives in a small world, it's bounded on the north, south, east, and west by Edith."[3]

The farmer also failed to see that his abundant crop really originated from God and not solely from his own efforts. Jesus did not describe him as "A man who worked his tail off, plowed from dawn to dusk, researched the best seed, was a master at fertilizing and soils, was a gifted harvester, and as a result, had a well-deserved huge harvest." Neither did Jesus mention that he is working on a soon-to-be-released masterclass and podcast. No, Jesus said, "The farm of a rich man produced a great crop."[4] God did it. It was an exceptionally good year of gentle rains, sunshine, and no adverse conditions. And he should have seen that. Wealth can surely bring to light our focus in life, and this guy failed the quiz.

He was so self-focused that he only sought out his own advice. He thought he had all the answers. Talking to oneself as a way of seeking advice can be risky, besides being a bit weird. For one, we may just get bad advice if the only person we ask is ourselves. Solomon, a smart guy himself, put it this way.

The way of a fool is right in his own eyes, but a wise man is he who listens to advice (Prov. 12:15 ESV).

We also miss out on engaging with others. In addition, the farmer never considers sharing his harvest with those in need! He never wonders who might need it more. He was already rich; the parable makes that clear. His only concern was for himself.

The farmer not only had a problem with being too self-focused; he was grossly self-absorbed.

Self-absorbed. The man's conversation (with himself) continues. "I'll say to myself, Self, you've done well! You've got it made. Take it easy and have the time of your life!" This guy had quite an over-inflated ego, didn't he? In short, he thought he was dang awesome. But here is the frightening thing, I battle with being all about myself as well. Perhaps you do too.

A man wrapped up in himself makes a very small bundle. —*Benjamin Franklin*

Our world is indeed ridiculously small if the only thing in it is us! This guy not only had over-stuffed barns but also an over-inflated view of himself. Having self-confidence can be a good thing. It is healthy to know our strengths, to be sure of our status as a child of God, deeply valued and loved by Him. But we can easily take it too far. When we are absorbed in only ourselves; that is when it's a problem.

Jesus asks us to consider others better than ourselves. And that, if we are honest, goes against our typical tendency. Yes, we all wrestle with our ego and all the baggage that comes with it.

All you need to know and observe in yourself is this: Whenever you feel superior or inferior to anyone, that's the ego in you. —*Eckhart Tolle*

The Bible speaks much about dying to our ego. It is what our journey of transformation is all about. Why? Jesus desires that our focus be on Him. And let's face it, we'd rather it be us! We can be more-than-just-a-little selfish. Jesus puts it rather plainly,

Unless a kernel of wheat falls to the ground and dies, it remains only a single seed. but if it dies, it produces many seeds (John 12:24).

If any want to become my followers, let them deny themselves and take up their cross and follow me (Mark 8:34 NRSV).

Jesus' words on dying to self are contrary to what we naturally admire. Independence and self-reliance are what we like, especially to us with a western mindset. We see rugged individualism and an I-can-do-it-myself attitude as strong traits. A combination of Dirty

Harry, Rey from Star Wars, and the Marlboro Man seem to be who we admire.[5] When have you seen the image of a sweet and humble soul selling products on a billboard? It doesn't happen for good reason—it wouldn't sell a product.

Our spiritual journey with Jesus should be less about greatness and more about dying than we want to admit. Our pride must go. We need to recognize when our ego is rearing its ugly head in our hearts and give it a boot out the back door. God desires humbleness.

Be completely humble and gentle; be patient, bearing with one another in love (Ephesians 4:2).

Meister Eckhart (1260-1328) said, "Spirituality has much more to do with subtraction than it does with addition." We can be rather obsessed with addition—securing financial security, achieving success, and earning status. We tend to admire the successful instead of the humble. Authentic spirituality is much more about letting go.

And what we need to let go of first and foremost is our ego. We are to let go of our need to be in control. We are to let go of our need to be seen and recognized by others.

Ouch. Was I right? Does this parable hurt a little?

Admitting we have an ego does hurt.

Entering the Story

As I pondered the setting of this parable, I couldn't help but remember a time much earlier in my life when I personally was the younger brother who did not get his fair share of the family inheritance!

My father had passed away. He was not the greatest father, but he was my dad, and I would miss him. Losing my father was hard, especially since I had already lost my mother. My father did not have much, but what he did have, he left to my brothers. It stung a little. Dad didn't leave me a thing.

What I did get was a wonderful time with my father, just the two of us, the very day before he died. We chatted all day, and he spoke wonderful words to me, most of them for the first time. I guess he knew he was near the end. He told me he was incredibly proud of who I was. That meant the world!

So, imagining myself in the scene of this parable was rather easy, I was transported back to that day. "Jesus, tell my brothers to give me my fair share!" I could relate. Jesus tenderly met me there and said, "Sam, let me tell you a story."

"A man hit it big with a great harvest. He tore down his barns and built huge ones. The farmer thought he had it all, all he could ever want. He got all the inheritance! Yet, he died miserably."

Jesus touched my heart with, "See what happens when you care more about yourself than you do Me? Yes, your brothers got the little your dad had. You got more! You had a good relationship with your dad."

"Better yet, I want us to have a great friendship! I want you to value our relationship over everything else! I love you! I love you more than you know!"

Well, safe to say, God's love for me became immensely more real after that conversation. And I did not realize I was still hanging on to a tiny bit of that pain from so long ago. Past pains have a way of sticking around, don't they?

I was able to let it go.

And guess what? It doesn't hurt anymore.

Living the Story

How do we know if our ego is too big? How do we know if we are too self-absorbed? You may want to ponder the following. Ask God to show you if these tendencies fit you in any way.

Attributes of an over-inflated ego:
- You enjoy pointing out other's flaws.
- You feel the need to win most every discussion.

- You often compare yourself to others.
- You find it hard to be glad for others' achievements.
- You talk about yourself much more than you genuinely listen to others.
- You set yourself impossible goals, then beat yourself up when you don't meet them.
- You find it hard to know when enough is enough.
- You most often direct the conversation and attention to you.
- You quickly defend yourself instead of listening to criticism for potential truth.
- You rarely help others, and when you do, you sure hope someone notices.

An honest reflection of these can be a sobering exercise. Ask God to make you more aware of how and when your ego becomes a hindrance. Ask God to develop in you a more humble and gentle heart and to help you become a person who genuinely cares for others.

Here is another sobering challenge. Consider these attributes of a person who is well on the path to a healthier ego.

Attributes of a healthy ego:
- When neglected or forgotten, even though it stings, you do not sulk from the oversight, but you find joy and contentment... that is dying to self.
- When your advice is disregarded or your opinion even ridiculed, yet you refuse to defend yourself...that is dying to self.
- When you don't refer to yourself in conversation or mention your accomplishments. Instead, you listen and don't mind going unnoticed...that is dying to self.
- When you see another succeed and prosper and you can honestly be glad for them and feel no envy, nor question what God is up to...that is dying to self.
- When you can receive correction from others, even from

someone of lower stature and you humbly listen, outwardly as well as inwardly…that is dying to self.

We are all going to die someday. For some, the slow road to dying will be an enormous struggle. For those who have learned to die along the way, physical death will be a gentle culmination of letting go that they practiced all their life. So, let's learn to die well now!

Having died to that which held us captive (Rom. 7:6 ESV).

Point of the Parable:

Are you the center of your world? If so, your world is much too small.

We want our fair share. We want what is coming to us.

Jesus said, "Fill your life up with God, not self."

We are neither superior nor inferior to anyone. We all need a Savior. We are all loved.

A Blessing for You, on Your Journey of Letting Go

May you know that God loves your truest self, the wonderful essence of who you are. God delights in you!

May you seek true humility that in no way cheapens the unique and strong person you are but allows it to grow and bloom.

May you be less and allow others to be more.

May you cease to be influenced by what others think of you or what you accomplish. May you tear that barn down board by board.

May you see and feel God's all-encompassing love for you. May you know there isn't a barn big enough to hold all of God's love…for you.

10

Being Ready

Yesterday is gone. Tomorrow has not yet come. We only have today. Let us begin. —Mother Teresa

"Be dressed ready for service and keep your lamps burning, like servants waiting for their master to return from a wedding banquet, so that when he comes and knocks, they can immediately open the door for him. It will be good for those servants whose master finds them watching when he comes. Truly I tell you, he will dress himself to serve, will have them recline at the table and will come and wait on them. It will be good for those servants whose master finds them ready, even if he comes in the middle of the night or toward daybreak. But understand this: If the owner of the house had known at what hour the thief was coming, he would not have let his house be broken into. You also must be ready, because the Son of Man will come at an hour when you do not expect him."

Peter asked, "Lord, are you telling this parable to us, or to everyone?"

The Lord answered, "Who then is the faithful and wise manager, whom the master puts in charge of his servants to give them their food allowance at the proper time? It

will be good for that servant whom the master finds doing so when he returns. Truly I tell you, he will put him in charge of all his possessions. But suppose the servant says to himself, 'My master is taking a long time in coming,' and he then begins to beat the other servants, both men and women, and to eat and drink and get drunk. The master of that servant will come on a day when he does not expect him and at an hour, he is not aware of. He will cut him to pieces and assign him a place with the unbelievers.

"The servant who knows the master's will and does not get ready or does not do what the master wants will be beaten with many blows. But the one who does not know and does things deserving punishment will be beaten with few blows. From everyone who has been given much, much will be demanded; and from the one who has been entrusted with much, much more will be asked" (Luke 12:35–48).

Listening to the Story

Be ready. Be ready for God to show up in your life.

This is the theme of this uncharacteristically long parable passage. Jesus first tells a story depicting servants being watchful and ready for their master's return. Peter then asks, "Jesus, was that just for us or for everyone?" I wonder what was behind Peter's question? Did Jesus sometimes tell special parables just for His inner circle of disciples? Did Peter think he was special? Or did he simply want to clarify his role?

Or maybe Peter wanted to clarify this master-going-away thing? By this time, the disciples deeply loved Jesus, and they didn't want Him going anywhere! Wait a minute, Jesus, is this for us? Are you going somewhere? You cannot leave us now! Peter must have felt confused and scared.

In asking his question, Peter does make it plain that Jesus just told a parable. "Is this parable for us or for everyone?" I for one am extremely glad Peter clarified this point. It is good to know that being "cut up into pieces," "beaten with many blows," or "thoroughly thrashed," as *The Message* puts it, is not a possible outcome! Let's get something straight, God does not or will not cut us up into pieces. We do enough of that on our own! We are hard enough as it is on us.

No, the thrashing was not intended to be taken literally. Parables are imaginative stories. Jesus often uses hyperbole to get our attention, and this is one of them. We use hyperbole all the time. "I'm so hungry I could eat a horse." "She's my guardian angel." "I've read that book a hundred times." And then for some reason, we want to take Jesus literally when He was storytelling.

As a way of answering Peter's question, Jesus asked another question and then elaborated on his story, gearing it especially for Peter and the other leaders. So, indirectly Jesus seems to tell Peter, "Yes, this is for you, and yes, in the future I will be gone, and you may feel alone at times. But always be looking for Me, for I am coming. In fact, I will always be with you." Knowing that helps to make a good leader.

Listen Up. Peter's question is a great one we should all ask. "Jesus, is this for me?" I think we know the answer is a resounding yes! This a great prayer as you approach every parable. Jesus, how is this for me?

Let's look at the very ending of Jesus' story to see how. Remember, a key to understanding a parable is to pay attention to the ending. Often, the ending is the key that unlocks the message mystery box.

The ending is, "To those who have been given much, much will be expected." Interesting. We have been given so much in our lives. Do you ever take inventory of all that has been given to you? Do you realize all that has proceeded you to form a wonderful foundation for you to enjoy?

We experience God's grace and love and mercy every day. God gives us family and friends. God gives us breath and life itself. God crafted His amazing creation, beautiful in all its magnificent and varied splendor, for us as a playground to care for. God gives us the ability to both laugh and cry—to feel a whole range of emotions.

God did not create a black and white world. No, God gives us an enormous spectrum of color, the feeling of touch, and the ability to hear sounds across a huge spectrum of frequencies. We hear the wind whistle through ponderosa pines, the crash of an ocean wave against a rocky shore, and the sweet sound of a child's giggle. We have the entirety of Scripture with a myriad of modern ways to study and enjoy it. We have been given Jesus and His Spirit that dwells within us. His Spirit prompts, leads, and loves us in a myriad of ways that I believe we have no clue about.

We indeed have been given much! We often take it all for granted. Yes, this parable and its message is for us.

Maybe you don't feel that way. Maybe you don't feel like you're anything special to God. Perhaps you feel terribly alone. At times, we all feel this way. Perhaps, you need to voice these feelings to Jesus now, and say, "Jesus, I feel so alone. Please be with me now. Let me be more aware of Your presence."

Cut Up. Let's go back to that "cut into pieces" elephant in the room, shall we? Some theologians think the word (*dichotomeo*) has more of a meaning of being "cut off," like when a society excludes a person for bad behavior.[1] Rabbinic teachings in the Mishnah (Jewish legal text) instructs that in certain circumstances people should be excluded from society. This practice has been historically carried out in certain strict Christian circles, often in cruel ways.

Some societies still practice this today. I had the privilege of visiting a remote and fascinating village named Siwa in western Egypt. It is situated within a large natural oasis, on the eastern fringes of the vast Sahara Desert. With its abundance of water, Siwa supports around 300,000 palm trees and 70,000 olive trees from 300 freshwater springs. Yet, just outside the village, in every direction is uninhabitable desert.

Living in Siwa is a unique people with their own language and customs. One such custom is that if anyone is caught stealing, they are paraded through town on a donkey cart for all to see. They are then taken outside of the village and left to fend for themselves, cut off from society. As you might guess, crime is extremely low in Siwa!

Even if one adheres to the "cut off" interpretation, it is still a harsh judgment and not to be taken literally. God in His infinite love always draws us into His embrace. He never pushes us away. Jesus said,

Whoever comes to me, I will never cast out (John 6:37 ESV).

That is great news! God is always and forever there for us! We will never be cast out! We never have to take that donkey cart ride of shame! God always wants to be with us. I guess the only question is, do we desire to be with Him?

The Message. Jesus longs for us to be eager and ready to be with him. Jesus wants us to be aware of and to enjoy His presence. I believe this is the message of the parable. In the NIV translation, *ready* is used four times in this passage. The words *expect* or *watch* are used three times. Being aware of God in our day, eagerly looking for His fingerprints of love, is a wonderful discipline. God is always near to us. Do we slow down enough to be aware of Him? (As a suggestion, Brother Lawrence's book, *The Practice of the Presence of God,* is a great resource).

When your eyes are open to God's presence in your life, you will always feel His love. —*Gift Gugu Mona*

One of our sons and his family live a half-day drive away—a short drive for eager grandparents! On one such drive, our daughter-in-law sent us a picture of our 2-year-old granddaughter standing in the window eagerly awaiting our arrival. You know how happy that made us feel? I pressed on the gas pedal a little firmer after seeing that picture! Sometimes, our granddaughter is waiting for us outside the house on their entry steps! It doesn't get any better than that.

I think our sweet little girl waiting on the steps is a wonderful picture of how our relationship with God should be. God desires for us to be on the steps eagerly awaiting Him. Or is it God on the steps awaiting *our* arrival? I think it goes both ways. Every beautiful relationship does, right?

Are we eager and ready for God to arrive in our life today? Are we on the steps? I wonder how often we miss God simply because we are not aware of His presence.

Father, help me be more ready for You and Your love. Help me realize I have been given so much from You. You desire for me to share all that I have with others. Help me to share a smile today. Help me to share Your love and mercy that You lavish on me!

Help me to be ready.

Entering the Story

I love watching Jesus.

He has a way of changing lives and captivating hearts through storytelling. I love His stories. As a disciple, I have a front row seat to most of them. Sometimes their message seems crystal clear, sometimes confusing, but I love listening to them either way. I am always captivated with the way He can speak to the hearts of a crowd.

This day He told several parables. He spoke of a servant of a household who served well and had the house in beautiful shape, ready for his master's return. His master was at a wedding. I thought that was kind of funny since Jesus was not married Himself, nor were most of us disciples.

I am a simple fisherman so I may not be the sharpest knife in the tool bag, yet I feel as though I understand what this parable means. As a fisherman I don't have servants, yet I certainly know the value of being ready. It's why we mend our nets to be ready for a night on the water. I was taught to always keep watch for just the right weather and water conditions. Sometimes we can spot a shoal of fish rise on the surface of the water. The water dances and looks like heavy rain is beating down on it. That's when you're glad your net is ready for a cast! Yes, I know the value of being ready.

Jesus seemed to be saying to me to be ready to be with God. Be ready for His daily arrival in my life and in my heart. God longs to be with me. Am I watchful and ready to be with Him? That was powerful imagery that touched my heart.

Suddenly, Peter interrupted my happy thoughts by asking Jesus a rather bold question. "Are you telling this parable for us or for everyone?" Seemed like Peter wanted to know if only us twelve disciples could have this kind of relationship with Jesus. I kind of shuddered as Peter asked that.

So, Jesus did what He so often does. He answered with another story! *Thanks Peter,* I thought to myself. Here goes another parable! Yet, deep down I was delighted at the chance to hear Jesus speak more. How I love Jesus!

This time Jesus spoke of not just a single servant in charge of a house, but of a chief servant, one who oversaw many servants. This story had even a sterner message, one which sent chills down my back. If the chief servant abused his position, he would be beaten or cut to pieces. Again, I thought, *thanks a lot, Peter!*

But as Jesus continued, I heard another message of love within it. God wants to show up and be with me. I think the message of the parable is, am I ready for God and His love?

If God is represented by the master, He sure seems demanding! I hear that loud and clear. Yet even this is incredibly special. God demands all of me! Not just part of me. God wants all my heart, all my soul, and all my strength. Who am I that God would desire me? How special that feels!

I instinctively went into prayer. Thank You, Father, for all that You have given me. Thank You for all the blessings and all that You have entrusted into my care. I have a family. I have people to mentor and disciple. I have so many people to love and to lead. Help me lead them to You!

Help me to always be ready for Your love in my life. Help me to spread that love. I want to hear You speak. Give me a pure heart. In fact, chop up my heart into pieces if necessary, until the only parts left are the ones that You desire! I desire a heart dedicated to loving You.

After my prayer, I lifted my head to see Jesus looking my way. He seemed so pleased. It was as if He knew exactly what I was praying.

Jesus came over to me and whispered in my ear. He said, "I am so pleased with you. I will always be with you. I love you! You heard the parable well."

Then, it hit me. I love watching Jesus. And Jesus loves watching me!

Living the Story

Sit with this parable and put yourself in the

Point of the Parable:

God shows up when we most expect Him.

Jesus said, "Be ready for Me right now."

Are we eager and ready to be with Jesus?

Yesterday is past. Tomorrow is yet to come. So, enjoy God in the present moment.

story. Try and imagine Jesus telling this parable just to you. Sit with it long enough to clearly hear a special word from Jesus.

- What words get your attention? What words may have been a struggle to hear? How did you resolve that? How would you summarize the key message of this parable?

- Consider how you can be more aware of God in your daily life. Do you compartmentalize your life into times when you feel God is present and times when you never think of him at all?[2] Try and have today be a sacred time of experiencing His presence as much as possible all through the day.

- Thank Jesus that He will never cast you away from His presence. Journal your thanks.

A Blessing for you, in Your Eagerness to be with God

May you feel the gentle, never stern love of your heavenly Father. May you know God desires oneness with you. As Jesus prayed for you; may you be one with God, one with Jesus, and one with His Spirit (John 17:20-23).

May you present yourself to God every day, eager to be near Him.

May you release everything else in your heart—any worry, any fear—that is taking up valuable room in your mind and soul besides the joy of knowing Him.

May you rejoice in the truth that God will never cast you out, never cart you off, never turn his back on you, but will always embrace you with His infinite love. You are marvelously loved!

11

Where's the Fruit?

With patience one can achieve what force never will.
—Clyde Lee Dennis

Now there were some present at that time who told Jesus about the Galileans whose blood Pilate had mixed with their sacrifices. Jesus answered, "Do you think that these Galileans were worse sinners than all the other Galileans because they suffered this way? I tell you, no! But unless you repent, you too will all perish. Or those eighteen who died when the tower in Siloam fell on them—do you think they were more guilty than all the others living in Jerusalem? I tell you, no! But unless you repent, you too will all perish."

Then He told this parable: "A man had a fig tree growing in his vineyard, and he went to look for fruit on it but did not find any. So, he said to the man who took care of the vineyard, 'For three years now I've been coming to look for fruit on this fig tree and haven't found any. Cut it down! Why should it use up the soil?'

"Sir," the man replied, "leave it alone for one more year, and I'll dig around it and fertilize it. If it bears fruit next year, fine! If not, then cut it down" (Luke 13:1–9).

Listening to the Story

Why do we suffer? Honestly, why does God allow us to suffer? You may have wondered about that.

Just this morning, I woke up with a swollen and throbbing big toe. I thought to myself, *I don't even remember bumping it, so why is it hurting?* I did go on a run yesterday, but I don't remember stubbing it. We often just want to know why, don't we?

In Jesus' day, it was common to blame suffering on sin. The thought was that a suffering person brought it onto themselves through wrongful living. This is the subject of discussion in our scene and the reason Jesus told the parable of an unproductive fig tree.

Isn't it refreshing that Jesus listened well? Some people were discussing a recent tragedy—Galileans were slaughtered by Romans, and their blood mixed in with sacrificial animal blood on an altar. That is horrible in the worst way!

We are not used to seeing blood today, unless you work in an emergency room, slaughterhouse, or you enjoy hunting. First century Galileans were more used to animal blood than we certainly are, but the thought of human blood on an altar intended for animal sacrifice had to be just as gruesome for them. Jesus listened, heard their hearts, and told a story.

The Backdrop. Pontius Pilate was the Roman governor over this distant region, far from Rome. His job was a precarious one, and he was often ruthless in crushing uprisings. Josephus states that Galileans were often the ones who revolted.[1,2] Perhaps Pilate had made a public display of yet another failed Galilean uprising. We don't really know. What we do know is the people were upset about it and wanted Jesus' view on it.

Jesus wanted to squash the idea that suffering is a result of sin. One would think the book of Job might have put that idea to bed for good, but no, it was still alive and well. What was Jesus' view?

"Do you think these Galileans suffered because of sin? I tell you, no!" That seems emphatic enough. But Jesus elaborates. He compares this tragic event to another incident where a stone tower collapsed and killed eighteen people. The fact that Jesus specifies the place (Siloam), and the number of people indicates to me this was also an actual event. It was yet another tragedy that caused people to question why.

To help them see that it is not sin that causes suffering, Jesus pointed out that we all mess up. Jesus twice said, "Unless you repent, you too will perish!" People often conclude that Jesus is referring to a final spiritual judgment and punishment here. I don't think so. Jesus was addressing actual events of people dying horrible deaths. So, it seems likely that Jesus wanted to warn them that the same thing could happen to them.

Jesus was wanting the revolt-loving Galileans to stop considering how to overthrow the kingdom of Rome and to embrace the kingdom of God that Jesus was ushering in. It's as though Jesus was saying, Stop being so concerned about the Romans. I don't want you to miss the goodness of God I desire for you. I don't want you to miss the love I have for you here and now. That is what Jesus' wanted them to see and enjoy.[3]

On another occasion, in John 9, Jesus also tried to squelch the idea that suffering is the result of sin. Jesus ran across a man blind from birth and was asked, "Who sinned, this man or his parents?" Jesus told them they were off base and proceeded to heal the man. He had him wash in the pool of Siloam. Sound familiar? This is the same Siloam, near where the tower fell, in the southern end of Jerusalem. This Siloam was a hotbed of sin and suffering, I guess! (I hope you caught my sarcasm!)

A Fig Tree. With this backdrop, let's get to the parable. Jesus told of an unproductive fig tree. The fig tree is within a vineyard. You cannot get any more symbolic of Israel, Jewishness, and their land than grapes and figs! Remember when Joshua sent spies into the promised land after escaping 400 years of slavery in Egypt? The spies brought back a huge cluster of grapes along with pomegranates and figs. These same fruits are still enjoyed in the Middle East today.

Jesus used the familiar fig tree in His story. Yet, the subtle twist is that a fig tree simply would not have been planted within a vineyard. Full grown fig trees are large and would consume too much ground water. The large canopy of the tree would create too much shade, and the figs would attract too many birds. All of this would interfere with the health of the vines.[4]

A fig tree may be planted on the edge of the vineyard, yet even still, any soil that can produce good grapes would be invaluable. I think this is what drove the owner to want to use the precious soil for additional vines if the fig tree was not producing figs. And maybe that fact is exactly part of the punch of the parable. The audience would think to themselves, yes, if that tree does not produce, get it out of there! It's a waste of good soil.

Isn't this parable weirdly intriguing, yet downright frustrating all at the same time—this get-the-ax-I've-had-enough stuff? Aren't we so glad God is nothing like the landowner? Yet, even in our story, the ax-loving owner shows patience and grace. He waits a good three years before first thinking it might be time to sharpen the ax. Then, he agrees to yet another year. If the landowner or the caretaker represent God, we are to realize that God is always patient with us even when we are at our worst. God is patient, even when we cannot seem to sprout a single, spiritual fig!

And here is the thing. Often, we tend to be our own landowner, frustrated at our own inadequacies![5] We can be so hard on ourselves, wondering when we will ever "produce" something special in our lives. Maybe it's time to allow God to speak to your heart, and say, "It's okay. I am happy to wait however many years it takes for you! In fact, you're pretty special the way you are right now!"

Have patience with all things, but, first of all with your-self. —*St. Francis De Sales*

The Message. God is always patient with us, even when we are not! God's view of time is so different than ours. Maybe God is fine if it even takes an eternity for us to become the best version of us. God is even fine if our journey of growth seems to contain more manure than tasty figs! God is fine with a slow pace, so we should be fine with who we are as well.

We are so hard on ourselves. We need to stop wondering if we are good enough, pretty, or strong enough. We are to simply enjoy His wonderful presence in our lives. We are to rest in the fact that God is lovingly patient with us.

We also need to stop deciding if other people are good enough! It's called judging, and Jesus had some words of advice on it, "Don't do it!" (Luke 6:37) So, let's stop judging others and de-ciding the quantity or quality of their figs.

Our lives are short. Our time for embracing His presence, for growth, and for making a difference is truly short. The only thing racing faster than the noise in our heads are the hands on the clock! Yet, God will not take an ax to us if we mess up again. His love for us is simply too big for that.

People can be lumped into two general categories: takers and givers. The fig tree was just taking nutrients from the soil and not giving anything back. God desires for us to give as much goodness back into the world as we take. Are you more of a giver or a taker?

One final especially important thought. If you are currently in a time of suffering, please realize an important thing—you did not do anything wrong! Not at all. Suffering is not some kind of pun-ishment from God, yet it is an invitation to go deeper with Him.

We can still struggle with this same question that these Galileans did. Why? Why are there tragic events globally? Why all the pain and suffering around me? And why do I have to suffer?

There are aspects of His love that we only learn through suffering. And God desires for you to deepen your enjoyment with Him. We are all on a journey of challenges and growth with much to learn along the way. But here is an amazing truth: God can be love to us within our suffering! God desires to walk with us through our pain, to be present with us.

Let's go back to the parable for something important. The caretaker of the fig tree said to the owner, "Leave it alone. I'll dig around it. I'll fertilize it!" Please, let me personally care for this tree, to nurture it, and see it through! It's hard to imagine a good gardener that doesn't get down on his hands and knees at some point and carefully tend the soil as a cook kneads dough. I picture this caretaker determined with all the skill he possesses to ensure growth. He adds nutrients. He removes the weeds. He spends whatever time is needed.

What a beautiful picture of where God is when we suffer! He never leaves us. He is deep in the manure with us, no matter how ugly or smelly it gets. His own hands are dirty with our grime and our filth. Why? Love. That's why. Why does God allow us to suffer? Love.

Well, my big toe is still throbbing.

Yet, after contemplating this parable I am choosing not to dwell on the pain nor the mystery of how it happened. The pain has less to do with my poor running form. (Even though I do resemble more of a flailing octopus than a sleek Kenyan marathoner.) My painful toe has more to do with being a fantastic reminder of my need for God's nurturing in my life.

So, I am choosing to smile. I am choosing joy with each painful step.

God never gives up on us, figs or no figs.

That makes my hurting toe just a little more bearable.

Entering the Story

"I too would perish," Jesus said.

Those words stung. Jesus seems to scorn us as we tell Him about some of our fellow Galileans that the Romans ruthlessly killed. Roman soldiers smeared the blood of our countrymen on our sacrificial altar! The thought of what they did to our friends makes my blood boil! Doesn't Jesus understand?

Living under Roman rule is worse than brutal. In Galilee, our lives aren't easy. We work hard, and we are a proud people. Yet, the Romans treat us harshly and tax us severely—just so they can build another building. Sometimes, it is more than we can tolerate.

I hate the Romans. There, I said it! Israel is the farthest eastern region under Roman occupation, so perhaps if we can mount an insurgency and drive them out, they would leave us alone for good. We were hoping that by telling Jesus of the men who were slaughtered at the hands of Pilate that He would become just as outraged. With Jesus as our leader, we could do anything!

We have never seen a man like Jesus. God hears His prayers. Jesus heals. He has even given sight to the blind! God is surely with Him! And Jesus has an immense following. If Jesus were to lead a Galilean revolt against Pilate, every man in Galilee would join in!

Our God defeated the mighty Egyptian army. God caused the fortified walls of Jericho to fall. Surely, God would help us defeat the Romans! This is our precious land promised to us! If Jesus is truly our Messiah, then it's time to go to battle and crown him King. Let's do this!

Yet, Jesus took our words a different way. He said we too will perish unless we repent from our feeble plans. He even called us sinners! That hurts.

Then Jesus told a story. A fig tree in need of the ax because it didn't produce any fruit. Yet, the caretaker, the master gardener, recommended more time. He gave it more tender care and showed even more patience. We could all relate to his story. We love our grapes and figs. Many of us have a direct part in growing fruit. It takes work. It takes patience. We all know that. And the thought of cutting down a fig tree is brutal. It's almost as brutal as the Romans cutting down our men.

Oh. I think I understand now. I look at Jesus, and I begin to cry. It would hurt to cut down a treasured fig tree, even if it does not produce fruit. In the same way, Jesus doesn't want me chopped down by the Romans.

And what's more, that is what Jesus wants me to do with my intolerance—to cut it down. Jesus wants me to enjoy Him as a Friend instead of devising ways to use Him! I need to grasp Jesus' message of love and not be so consumed with revenge and hate.

Jesus, I need your tender gardening in my heart. I have so far to go.

I need Your patience so I can be patient. I need Your compassion so I can have compassion. I want Your love so I too can love. I want to start by loving myself. Allow me to realize the depth of Your love for me.

What needs pruning is my heart of hate!

Living the Story

Imagine Jesus telling you this parable. If you don't care for figs, imagine your favorite fruit tree. Imagine tasting that delicious fruit! Imagine how frustrating it would be to have to cut down that tree.

- Who is your worst

Point of the Parable:

God is always patient with us. We need to be as well.

Where is God in the awfulness of pain and suffering? God is here lovingly tending to your heart, inviting you to go deeper with Him.

Jesus said, "I dig and toil, so you can rest and flourish."

critic? Is it your parents, your boss, or a particular person? Is it you?

• Ponder the critical words you hear. Ponder the self-doubting words that often come into your mind. Now imagine Jesus telling you just the opposite.

• What needs to be cut down from within your heart? What needs to be cultivated and nurtured into growth?

• Thank God for His immense patience with you. Journal your thoughts.

A Blessing for You, as Your Roots Grow Deeper into His Love

May the gift of God's immense love settle your heart as you quiet yourself before Him. May you receive His love; enabling you to let go of any judgment toward yourself and others. May you know that God thinks you are lovely, right now.

May you rejoice that God is always patient with you, even when you are not.

May God grant you peace even amid suffering. May Jesus, deeply wounded for you, take your wounds, and lovingly be with you. May you have joy, that only comes by facing, not ignoring, your pain. May you see you did nothing wrong.

May you become less of a fighter, more of a lover, less of a taker, more of a giver.

May you know that Jesus will care for you with gentle hands. May you rest in that truth.

12

Little into a Lot

If you cannot be a lighthouse, be a candle. —Arab Proverb

Then Jesus asked, "What is the kingdom of God like? What shall I compare it to? It is like a mustard seed, which a man took and planted in his garden. It grew and became a tree, and the birds perched in its branches."

Again, he asked, "What shall I compare the kingdom of God to? It is like yeast that a woman took and mixed into about sixty pounds of flour until it worked all through the dough" (Luke 13:18–21).

Listening to the Story

Little things. Sometimes it's all we need. Sometimes little things are all we can do. Often, just a little initiative of love has a big impact to change a mood, to encourage, or to foster growth.

A mustard seed is one of the smallest of all seeds. There are a few that are smaller. No matter. In Jesus' day, a mustard seed was a metaphor for extremely small.[1] It meant as tiny as you could get.

Yeast is a similar metaphor for little. It sure doesn't take much yeast to turn dough into a growing, bubbling mound of goodness that when baked, will nourish and delight. "A little yeast works through the whole batch of dough," states Galatians 5:9.

In these two little parables Jesus uses tiny things that trigger big results. A tiny seed grows into a plant big enough that birds can perch on its branches. A little yeast can turn a large amount of dough into enough bread to feed and nourish a lot of people. Rest and nourishment are the result.

These stories are also about the ordinary. A man planting a garden and a woman baking bread—you cannot get more ordinary than that. These stories had to touch the hearts of these rural people. Every day, women baked bread. Season after season, men planted and harvested gardens.

I long to accomplish a great and noble task, but it is my chief duty to accomplish small tasks as if they were great and noble. —Helen Keller

Let's see if we can understand how these stories would have fallen on the ears of their original hearers. We will see that Jesus used familiar items, yet he used them in delightfully odd ways.

Yeast. Yeast (*zume*) in that day was like sourdough starter of today. Each day, after bread was baked, a little dough was kept aside and allowed to ferment. This is not a cute little yellow bag of powdered yeast kept in a refrigerator door.[2] If you've ever worked with sourdough starter, you know it can be fun, but you also know it can be challenging. It can go bad on you, turning moldy and smelly.

To the Jews, yeast often (yet not always) symbolized something bad. They were to clear it from their households at Passover (Ex. 12:19). Jesus used it to describe the hypocrisy of the Pharisees as in, "Be on your guard against the yeast of the Pharisees" (Luke 12:1). So, for Jesus to use yeast to describe God's kingdom might have been a bit edgy. I kind of like it that Jesus was edgy.

But let's remember that Jesus boldly declared Himself as,

"Living bread" (John 6:51). One of the temple sacrifices (Lev. 7:13) was "thick loaves of bread made with yeast." So, yeast clearly did not always represent something bad. Still, it must have caused his audience to pause in thought.

What about the quantity of bread baked in Jesus' story? It was huge! It is estimated at 40-60 pounds. I have mixed and poured a little cement in my day. Rest assured, after lugging around a few 60-pound sacks of dry-mix cement, I'm worn out and my back tells me about it the next day!

So, this amount of dough was far too much for one woman to knead on her own, and the yield would be far too much for just a few people to eat. The image Jesus wanted to create is clearly one of extravagance![3] A woman with a tiny amount of yeast bakes a large feast!

Sometimes the little opportunities that fly at us each day have the biggest impact. —Danny Wallace

Mustard. Mustard was typically grown in a field and not in a small garden. Mustard shrubs are fast growing and can easily invade an orderly vegetable garden. Some suggest it also went against Rabbinic law (drawn from Lev. 19:19), but that is probably an overstatement.[4] Yet, for Jesus, in His story, to have a man plant mustard in a garden would be a little edgy, yet again.

What's more, that little seed growing into a tree? Not so fast! Mustard is a plant, growing shoulder-high at best, with bright yellow flowers. It's not a tree. There is a tree that can occasionally be found near riverbeds in the Jordan Valley, called a mustard or toothbrush tree (*Salvadora Persica*). Sticks from this tree are still used as natural toothbrushes in Africa. This could have been what Jesus was referring to, but I don't think so because the seeds of this tree are not so tiny, and it's not likely one would plant a tree for producing toothbrushes in their garden.

I believe Jesus was more likely referring to true mustard plants

(*Brassica nigra* or *alba*) that were commonly planted in fields. The seeds of this plant are indeed tiny—only 1-2 mm—and were used as a seasoning.

What we must realize here is that to a western mindset, accuracy within a story is especially important. To ancient Hebrews, it was not. Stories were told to relay a message and it was perfectly fine to use hyperbole to make a point even stronger.

So, what was Jesus up to with His edgy stories here? Jesus intended to get His listeners to think a bit. Yeast and mustard seeds were certainly small things, somewhat insignificant, and a little obscure. And the way Jesus used them was possibly even a bit scandalous.

Jesus made these stories unconventional to make a point. As a result, it made the spiritual elite more than a little nervous. It often takes a maverick to significantly change things! Jesus was just that—a maverick of a rabbi. And Jesus certainly changed the course of history.

It also reminds me of His twelve motley disciples. They certainly were not the brightest and best of their day. They were rural village boys with a hated tax collector thrown in (like yeast?) for good measure. Yet, these twelve characters would carry forth Jesus' message throughout the known world. Jesus kneaded that small band of boys into men that would later accomplish something hugely significant. *Pew Research* estimates there are 2.3 billion Christians in the world today. Not bad, boys!

The Message. So, what do these two parables teach? Perhaps Jesus wanted to break their expectation of what His new kingdom would be. Jesus Himself would simply not accomplish what they were hoping for. Jesus was not going to lead a coup and overthrow the mighty Romans.

In fact, Jesus' life in many ways would not look like a success at all. Jesus would be brutally killed. For these people, Jesus would very soon be dead. Let's face it, Jesus wasn't what they had hoped for.

And that is a lesson for us. God often works differently than we expect! We need to look for God in the little things. We need to look for Him in the obscure things. Maybe God shows up all the time in the everyday! I'm convinced He does. It's up to us to notice.

In fact, God is even in our yucky yeast! God is with the hurting when they are hurting the most. God is in the present moment if we take the time to look and listen.

God is a god of the present. God is always in the moment, be that moment hard or easy, joyful or painful.
—Henry Nouwen

I once had a dreadful experience of a man unexpectedly dying right before my eyes. I was playing left field on our softball team. Ken was the center fielder who was a gifted athlete—an awesome batter and fielder. As we were running in from the outfield after an inning, Ken suddenly collapsed. A friend and I tried to resuscitate him for what felt like hours until an ambulance arrived. My friend did the CPR while I sat there and tried to encourage Ken to somehow wake up. Ken never did.

We would learn later that he suffered a brain aneurism which killed him quickly. He was pronounced dead on arrival at the hospital. It sure didn't feel like God was in that moment, that's for sure.

Days later, the nurse that treated him in the ER found me and asked how I was doing. I said, "I'm doing okay." She told me, "You did everything you could." I nodded and said thanks. She told me a second time, "Sam, you did everything you could." Once again, I said, "Thanks." Then, she looked deep into my eyes with her own piercing blue eyes, made sure I didn't look away, and once again said, "Sam, you did everything you could."

At that moment, I burst into tears, sobbing in her arms like a little boy. She knew I needed to hear that. She knew I needed to let go of the inner pain of feeling like I let a man die. And you know what? That is where God was! God used her three tiny, little questions to create a colossal amount of healing.

Jesus wants us to know the power of a little thing. Jesus wants us to know that a little act of kindness can heal a heart that is hugely hurting.

We sometimes underestimate the influence of little things. —*Charles W Chestnutt*

As I write this, it is the anniversary of 9/11 in America. That moment was horrendous for so many. Father Martin, a Jesuit priest was at Ground Zero in the aftermath. He shares, "As I looked around at the rescue workers, I thought, what is God like? God is like the firefighters who rush into a burning building to save someone. That's how much God loves us."

Yes, God is like a firefighter rushing into a burning building against all odds. God is like a caring nurse who couldn't save a man from a brain aneurism, but who could heal another man's wounded heart. God is like a tiny seed. God is even like a batch of sourdough starter, sitting in a jar on the kitchen counter. You can miss Him. Or you can notice His fragrance and watch Him work!

God most often shows up as a little thing, in the little things that mean so much.

Entering the Story

Jesus saw His mother Mary making bread countless times. In fact, the baking of bread wasn't the work of an individual, so he probably even helped her.

The daily task of baking bread was not a quick one. Grain was ground into flour by hand using small millstones. The flour was mixed into dough. Yeast was added to the mix and left to rise. Each day, a fire was started in a clay oven and stoked into embers creating just the right temperature for baking. The process took hours.[5]

Jesus saw Joseph planting a garden, year in and year out. Along with carpentry, Joseph would have surely worked whatever garden they had to grow vegetables. Any gardener knows firsthand the work involved. As a boy, Jesus would have surely taken part in the family gardening.

Jesus must have loved freshly baked bread from His mom. Who doesn't? Who knows, maybe the bread was even flavored with mustard! Jesus told stories from His own everyday life experiences. We do the same, don't we? Yeast and mustard seeds would have been vivid memories for Jesus.

Listening to Jesus tell stories based on his fond childhood memories brought up a memory of my own of my mom. I did not have my mom long. She died when I was only six years old. Yet, a memory came up so I thought it must be significant, and I enjoyed remembering it.

I was playing at my mother's feet while she was ironing. I was incredibly young. Yet I clearly remember enjoying being at her feet while she was doing what moms do. She was caring for her family. She was doing the mundane, so we could have clothes on our backs and food in our bellies.

Mom kept scooting me away from being directly under the ironing board, where the hot iron could potentially fall on me. But I wanted to be right next to her, so I kept crawling back to her feet. After a while, mom picked me up and held me with one arm while she ironed with the other hand. That surely wasn't the most efficient way to iron a shirt. But it was the best way to care for a beloved child in the moment.

Thank you, Jesus, for the special memory of being with my mom. Thank You, Jesus, that You spoke from the memories of Your mom and dad. Thank You that You were wonderfully human.

Thank You that You call me to do the little things that I can do.

Help me love people well by doing little acts of kindness. Help me see who needs a special hello or a big smile. Let me notice who needs a bigger than normal tip. Let me see who needs me to slow down and offer up a sincere, "How are you?" And give me the grace to listen well.

Jesus, please cultivate in me a growing ability to love others well. God, may Your love spread like a weed.

Living the Story

After pondering this parable, you may want to relish a special childhood memory of your own.

- With a prayerful heart, ask God to help you remember the details of a special childhood memory. Journal your memory. Recall every loving moment. What were you thinking and feeling? Why was it so special to you? Who was there? Feel the joy in your heart once again. Thank God for that beautiful event in your life.

> **Point of the Parable:**
>
> **Big things are little things done with a lot of love.**
>
> Little things. At times, it's all we need. At times, it's all we have the strength for.
>
> Jesus said, "Be like a tiny seed or a little yeast and allow Me to do the growing."
>
> God often shows up in little acts of love.

- Now, once again go to your special memory, and this time ask Jesus (with an open heart to hear from Him) what He was doing behind the scenes that helped make it so special. Where was He? How did He help orchestrate that moment just for you? What was He feeling at the time?

- Journal what you hear and praise Him for what He did for you in that special moment. Praise Him for His infinite love for you!

What small, yet significant acts of kindness do you enjoy doing for others? Ask God to lead you into ways of doing this more.

A Blessing for You, a Doer of Little Things

May you take delight in the myriad of little things that happen all throughout your day. May you see God in those things. May you feel God's acceptance and pleasure in you.

May you feel God's presence in the mundane, the silly, and even in the yucky things. May you see the boy Jesus helping His mom carry a sack of flour. May you picture Jesus gardening with His dad. Notice the joy they share together.

May you enjoy the sweet memories you have of a loving parent, aunt/uncle, grandparent, or close friend. May you create special memories for others.

May you know God loves you even if you feel small and insignificant. May God meet you in whatever you are doing right now. May you take a moment to enjoy a special little thing just for you.

13

Time for a Feast

God comes to those who come to God with their lives
just as they are. —Thomas Keating

*Then Jesus said to his host, "When you give a luncheon
or dinner, do not invite your friends, your brothers or sisters, your relatives, or your rich neighbors; if you do, they
may invite you back and you will be repaid. But when you
give a banquet, invite the poor, the crippled, the lame, the
blind, and you will be blessed. Although they cannot
repay you, you will be repaid at the resurrection of the
righteous."*

*When one of those at the table with him heard this, he
said to Jesus, "Blessed is the one who will eat at the feast
in the kingdom of the righteous."*

*Jesus replied: "A certain man was preparing a great ban-
quet and invited many guests. At the time of the banquet,
he sent his servant to tell those who had been invited,
'Come, for everything is now ready.' But they all alike
began to make excuses. The first said, 'I have just bought
a field, and I must go and see it. Please excuse me.'
Another said, 'I have just bought five yoke of oxen, and
I'm on my way to try them out. Please excuse me.' Still
another said, 'I just got married, so I can't come.'*

"The servant came back and reported this to his master. Then the owner of the house became angry and ordered his servant, 'Go out quickly into the streets and alleys of the town and bring in the poor, the crippled, the blind and the lame.' 'Sir,' the servant said, 'what you ordered has been done, but there is still room.' Then the master told the servant, 'Go out to the roads and country lanes and compel them to come in, so that my house will be full. I tell you, not one of those who were invited will get a taste of my banquet'" (Luke 14:15–24).

Listening to the Story

A great meal with friends is truly a special time. The delightful tastes plus rich conversation becomes a much greater experience than the collective sum of the food and fun. There is something special about intentionally preparing your favorite dish for those you love. You want it exactly right. Conversely, it is an honor to be invited to such an event.

We each have unspoken dinner-party protocols we follow. Maybe you prefer your guests to not arrive too early. It's a little embarrassing to be caught frantically vacuuming the carpet and scurrying around the kitchen. You probably don't want them arriving too late either, for you timed the meal preparation to be at its best when you told them to come.

Perhaps its customary for guests to bring flowers, a beverage, or part of the meal. The host may use their best china, play special music, have a fire crackling in the fireplace, or candles burning on a perfectly decorated dinner table—all to create a special setting for sharing hearts.

The Protocols. The culture at the time of Jesus had its own party protocols. It may seem odd to us that in the parable, servants went out to round up the guests. But in that day, you fixed the day of an event and then guests were personally summoned to come when everything was ready.[1] No one had a watch back then. A banquet meal would take countless hours to prepare. Its completion was hard to predict.[2]

Important and elite guests would try and time their arrival to be last, to make a grand entrance. Maybe that hasn't changed over the centuries!

Even today, expected arrival times in the Middle and Far East are quite different than in the West. When I attended my first wedding in Pakistan, I arrived at the time eloquently printed on the fancy invitation. That makes sense, doesn't it? I was the first one there, by hours!

The hosts wondered why I came so early! By the time the other guests arrived, I was worn out from sitting so long and trying my best to not appear bored silly. When I left, well after midnight, I was the first to leave! I had to explain myself to the groom later!

In Jesus' day, there weren't printed invitations, nor did you know the exact timing of an event, but what you did know is that, if you were invited, you must go! To refuse offered hospitality was a grave insult. You could do everything else wrong, but you simply had to be there! To not attend would shame the host.[3] Only the best of reasons could keep someone away. So, the obvious conflict in Jesus' parable of the "great" banquet was the not-so-great attitude of the invited guests!

The Excuses. Let's look at the reasons given for not accepting the invitation and see if they measure up. The first two, "I have just bought a field. I must go see it" and "I have just bought five yokes of oxen" seem poor at best. Before one buys a field or animals, they have probably already seen them. The third one, just getting married, is a little more reasonable. Yet, both a wedding and a great banquet would take considerable planning, so it is odd both events happened to land on the same day.

Interestingly, Deuteronomy 20:5–7 allows for a man who has just built a new house and not dedicated it, planted a vineyard and not yet enjoyed its fruit, or who has just become engaged to be excluded from battle.[4] These interestingly mimic our parable excuses. Deuteronomy 24:5 states that a man who is just married to be excluded from service. Other Jewish writings (Maccabeus and the Mishnah)[4] also include similar references.

So, is Jesus using these similar excuses as a way of saying, "You have heard it said...but I say...?" Or is it more the heart behind the excuses is what makes them poor? Jesus does seem to play off this familiarity for His story. And it was probably far different to be excused from a battle, where one might be killed never to see his bride again, than attending a friend's banquet.

The Message. Some theologians relate these poor excuses to general themes of how we can ignore God in our lives, such as, when career (field), passions (oxen), or homelife (bride) take priority over God. The point is that even good things can keep us from experiencing the best thing—a deep relationship with God. That is indeed an important truth and something we all need to remember and balance in our lives.

Let's look a bit deeper. Jesus tells His story after He instructs the real host that he should invite the underprivileged and not just his elite friends. In the parable, the host invites the underprivileged after his preferred guests are all no-shows. The point is, Jesus wants us to hang out with those in need, not exclusively our close friends or the muckety-mucks we want to impress.

In the parable, the host is forced to invite anyone and everyone so the food does not go to waste. And maybe that is indeed the point. God invites everyone into His presence. Not a morsel of God's love ever goes to waste! God invites those who we would expect—namely us. (I mean, who wouldn't invite us!) Yet, God also invites those that might surprise us. You know, the folks we wouldn't want to socialize with!

In fact, isn't Jesus' exhortation to party with the poor, the crippled, and the blind an obvious reflection of who Jesus mostly mingled with? When Jesus first announced that His work would begin, He read from Isaiah, and proclaimed that He came for the poor, the prisoner, the blind, and the oppressed (Luke 4:16–21).

You see, God desires for everyone to have a relationship with Him. God does not see social, racial, or political divides like we do. God sees beyond any divide. God loves us all.

We (all) are called to an everlasting preoccupation with God. —A.W. Tozer

Let's look closely at the ending to uncover even more meaning. Jesus makes two important points. First, the host's house will be full. Whenever I travel across continents, I am overwhelmed at the massive amount of people that call the same big ball home. I am always left breathless at the thought that God knows and loves us all. God is knocking on each heart at every moment in every place—inviting us all to a love feast. God is truly awesome.

But, what about the final words of the parable, "Not one of those (originally) invited will get a taste of my banquet." Why does the host have to go and get so harsh and angry? Is this the same person who compelled anyone to come? The intent of the word compel (*anankazo*), is not one of force, but one of urging. God is always the gentlemen. He never forces Himself on us. Yet God gently and continually urges us all into His love.

I personally believe the host's harsh words to his original invitees were Jesus' way of making a strong point—we should honor God's invitation. Any excuse to not be with God is a lame excuse. And we need to be more aware of God's quiet and consistent invitations into His presence.

God is continually nudging and urging us to draw close to Him. His nudges are all around. All that we see, smell, and taste are an invitation. God is everywhere—in the innocent smile of a child and in the rich aroma of freshly brewed expresso. God is in the excitement you feel when you are enjoying your favorite activity. What is sad is that we often miss His invitations into love.

To fall in love with God is the greatest romance; to seek him is the greatest adventure; to find him, the greatest human achievement. —Saint Augustine

What keeps us from God's presence is our own lack of awareness or flat-out disinterest.

Perhaps after contemplating this parable, you will appreciate a meal with friends even more, knowing it is a picture of how God longs for time with us. What an overwhelming idea—and it's true—God longs for time with you!

Perhaps, you will desire to be with a broader spectrum of people. Perhaps you will invite those who need a taste of the presence of God.

It's fine and wonderful to enjoy a meal with those we treasure. More importantly, we are to treasure time with God.

It's time to drop the lame excuses.

Entering the Story

There is so much to do. We have invited Jesus, the young and exciting new rabbi from Galilee to come to a banquet at our house.

We have prepared and cooked a prized lamb. It took us all day roasting it over an open fire. We have prepared grapes, dates, and pomegranates. We baked fresh bread. The aroma of the food is delightful. We made sure we had plenty of well-aged wine. It's so much work, but we are excited to host and honor Jesus.

What a treat to have Jesus in our own home! We want it to be perfect. We also invited some of our dearest friends. They too are thrilled to enjoy an evening with Jesus. What will Jesus be like? Will He like us? What will He teach us? I am hoping we will engage in wonderful conversation. I could not be more excited!

The evening is finally here, and guests are starting to arrive, including Jesus and His friends. Jesus humbly makes His way to a spot away from the banquet table in the corner of the room. I would have none of that. I take His hand and lead Him to a seat to my right, the most honored position at the table. In my excitement, I didn't even realize that I chased away a close friend who was reclining at that position!

Here at my table was Jesus, sitting with me and my closest friends. As host, I take the head position next to Jesus. It all was going as planned! We begin by offering each guest water to wash their hands. Then we bring out the meal, each course as I had planned it. I'm hoping Jesus is pleased. I guess I'm also selfishly hoping Jesus is impressed with all that I've done to honor Him.

I notice Jesus give a nod to others who were arriving—folks I didn't know and didn't invite. There was a man with a cane and a deformed leg. He was creating quite a scene as he was knocking into people. There was a blind woman, led by another lady inching her way into the crowded courtyard, also causing a ruckus. *Why did such a rag-tag bunch of undesirables show up,* I wondered?

I think Jesus read the healthy dose of displeasure on my face. Jesus then spoke, quoting from our beloved book of Isaiah[5]:

> **On this mountain the Lord of Hosts will make for all peoples a feast of rich food, a feast of well-aged wine, of rich food full of marrow, of aged wine well refined. And he will swallow up on this mountain the covering that is cast over all peoples, the veil that is spread over all nations** (Isaiah 25:6–7 ESV).

Was Jesus just comparing my dinner party to the future Great Feast in heaven we all anticipate? What a compliment!

Then it occurred to me. I think I realize what Jesus is saying.

113

Jesus came for all people—even the sketchy ones that just entered my house! Jesus then told a parable illustrating that a true host isn't so exclusive in who he invites. His parable sort of rips at my heart. All my intentions to impress Jesus only brought his not-so-subtle rebuke.

Yet, the shame I felt soon changed to appreciation as He looked at me and said these words.

"You meant so well, My son. You did so much to honor and serve Me. Thank you. Can you now show that same love to those you normally ignore? Can you love the seemingly unlovely? Can you see that they are equally as beautiful a creation as you?"

Jesus then told me He loved me just the way I am. Tears well up in my eyes as He spoke, "I love you."

Jesus did teach that night. He taught me who to invite to a meal. He taught me what love really means. And He taught me that He loves me.

Living the Story

Take time with this parable. As you do, ponder what the perfect meal with friends looks like for you.

- Remember one of your favorite meals with close friends. What made it so special? What did you talk about? What made the quality of the conversation so rich?

- Now imagine Jesus was at that same

Point of the Parable:

What keeps us from God is indifference, packaged in a lame excuse.

We think heaven is where we will finally and freely enjoy God. That's just an excuse for not being close to God now.

Jesus said, "Go everywhere and urge people to come. I want a full house!"

God invites us all into a deep friendship.

dinner party. Was He pleased? How did He join in? What did He say to you?

- Can you think of people that you would not normally entertain at your house that you now wish to have over?
- Thank God for His incredible love. Journal your thoughts.

A Blessing for You, as You Host Jesus

May you hear and accept God's invitation into His presence at this very moment. God treasures time with you. May you arrive early and stay late. May you delight in being with God throughout your day.

May you give your heart fully to Him—all that you enjoy, all your dreams, and all your passions—may you lay it all at His feet. May you be most content with God's love and grace in your life.

May you drop every excuse to not be with God. May you treasure your time with God as much as He does with you.

14

It'll Cost You

The Christian must understand that he is given life, not to keep it for himself, but to spend it for others.

—William Barclay

"For which of you, desiring to build a tower, does not first sit down and count the cost, whether he has enough to complete it? Otherwise, when he has laid a foundation and is not able to finish, all who see it begin to mock him, saying, 'This man began to build and was not able to finish.'

"Or what king, going out to encounter another king in war, will not sit down first and deliberate whether he is able with ten thousand to meet him who comes against him with twenty thousand? And if not, while the other is yet a great way off, he sends a delegation and asks for terms of peace.

"So therefore, any one of you who does not renounce all that he has cannot be my disciple" (Luke 14:28–35).

Listening to the Story

I wonder if Jesus whittled. As a carpenter, I cannot help but think he may have done a little whittling while sitting around a fire at night chatting with friends.

I imagine those chats were often pure fun. Other times, they may have been hard. Jesus informed His friends that following Him would come at a cost. It may, in fact, cost a disciple everything.

His words just before He spoke these two parables were brutally harsh.

Large crowds were traveling with Jesus and turning to them he said: "If anyone comes to me and does not hate his father and mother, his wife and children, his brothers and sisters—yes, even his own life—he cannot be my disciple. And anyone who does not carry his cross and follow me cannot be my disciple" (Luke 14:25–27).

Yikes! Did Jesus just say that? Jesus' words must have sent some folks running for the exits—for the quickest trail back home! Jesus often is different than what we expect Him to be! Jesus, at times, was wonderfully tender and compassionate; yet at other times, He was strikingly abrasive with His words, almost as if He wanted to chase people away.

Our natural tendency is to judge our worth by our successes, at least a little. And we can feel successful if we have significant friends or a lot of followers! If Jesus would have been like you and me, He should have been pleased with a large crowd of admirers. Yet, it's as though Jesus saw the crowd and deliberately tried to whittle it down.

Jesus seemingly wanted only dedicated followers. Jesus desires disciples who can genuinely live sacrificially. And, by the way, Jesus is quite different than you or me!

The terrible thing, the almost impossible thing, is to hand over your whole self—all your wishes and precautions—to Christ. —C.S. Lewis

Jesus' words of hating our parents are not to be taken literally. They are strong words intended to make a strong point that our devotion to Jesus should be our highest priority.

We also do not need to carry an actual wooden cross around as a sign we follow Jesus. Funny, I have seen a man do just this. He dragged around a large, bulky wooden cross to strike up a conversation for evangelism. He did get noticed in coffee shops; I grant him that! Jesus used the cross—a symbol of death—to let us know our life should be one of surrender.

Let's look deeper at the two parables. Jesus used examples from everyday life, things that would have been familiar to the people, to teach a truth that was not so familiar.

A Tower and a Battle. The tower in Jesus' story was probably a vineyard tower.[1] Family vineyards were often equipped with a tower from which one could keep watch. It was common for thieves to try and steal grapes just before harvest. So, building watchtowers would have been a familiar event (Isa. 5:2).

Jesus worked as a carpenter, perhaps many years before His three-year ministry outlined in the Gospels. Carpenters like Jesus built furniture and yokes. They also built structures. It's very likely that Jesus had firsthand experience with client's aspirations bigger than their savings, starting then stopping a building project. Perhaps, Jesus even built a half-finished tower for someone.[2]

In the first parable the outcome of poor planning was a little mockery. The words, "This man began to build and was not able to finish," rhyme in the Greek. It suggests to me it may have been a common expression. The rhyming reminds me of grade-school teasing. Think of a child singing, "You can't finish what you started! You can't finish what you started!"

A little good-natured ribbing from friends can be somewhat fun in our culture today. But, in first-century Mediterranean culture, being shamed was not a laughing matter. To "lose face," is a common expression in the Middle East, and one avoids it at all costs. So, the teasing within the first parable probably had a much worse consequence than it would to us.

The result of poor planning in the second parable, however, is worse still. Losing a battle could mean thousands might perish and the loss of a kingdom. Proverbs 24:6 instructs that one should only go into battle after seeking out wise guidance from trusted counselors. A Qumran scroll (11Q19, 68.1–21) gives instructions for how many soldiers to send out for battle in various situations, yet only after seeking advice and guidance from the high priest.[3]

The Message. These two parables have a unique grammatical structure. They pose a question that would suggest an obvious negative reply. Jesus asked, "Who would build a tower and not first consider the cost?" and "What king would go to battle before carefully considering if he could win?" The answer to both in the mind of the listener would have been, "Nobody…no one would do such a thing…certainly, not me!"

So, the high-level message of these parables appears to be that nobody should think being a disciple of Jesus is going to be easy!

> Salvation may be free, but it's not cheap.
> —T. W. Manson

Let's also consider the timing of when Jesus spoke these two little parables. Jesus was on His way to die and He knew it. He wanted His loved ones to know the cost of being a disciple. For martyrs over the last two-thousand years, following Jesus has cost them their lives.

Let's remember one such martyr whose name was Maximilian. Maximilian was born in Poland in 1894. At the age of twelve, he dedicated his life to God. He became a priest and during the 1920s and 1930s, he travelled widely, spreading the gospel in Japan and India. Poor health forced him to return to his native Poland in

1936. The timing could not have been worse.

When the Nazis invaded his country, Maximilian was given the chance to earn enhanced rights and privileges in exchange for signing a document recognizing his German ancestry. Maximilian refused. He also could have had a much easier time under the occupation had he given up publishing religious texts. His writings were critical of the Nazis, so in 1941, he was arrested and sent to the Auschwitz death camp. Maximilian was prisoner number 16670.

In Auschwitz, Maximilian kept serving as a priest, even though this meant receiving regular beatings. Things went from bad to worse when ten prisoners escaped the camp. To deter other such attempts, the Nazis picked ten prisoners to lock up in a barracks until they would die of starvation. One of the men chosen begged for his life, crying out that he had a wife and children. Maximilian offered to take his place. That's right, Maximilian willingly chose that barracks! So, along with nine others, he was locked in, left to die a slow, agonizing death.

Inside, Maximilian led the men in prayer. They lasted two agonizing weeks, and Maximilian was the last to die. What about the man who Maximilian replaced in that barracks? He survived Auschwitz, lived to be 93 years old, and dedicated much of his life to telling the world about Maximilian's act of sacrifice.

For most of us, following Jesus will not cost us an early death. Yet, there is still a cost. What will it cost us to truly live a life of intimacy with Christ? For one, it should mean you lose your self-centeredness. God asks us to die to our personal desires over His. God asks us to follow His will over ours and to consider others better than us. This means sacrifice and surrender.

It is told that when Queen Elizabeth was a little girl, she was forbidden to do something she wanted to do. She became angry and blurted out, "I am a princess, and I will do what I want!"

Her grandfather, King George said, "You *are* a princess and that is the very reason why, for your entire life, you will never be able to do as you like."[4] Queens live in luxury yet are bound in service to their country. Jesus was mocked as a king, a crown of thorns was pressed into his head, and He suffered a miserable death. As daughters and sons of that King, we are also to live a selfless life.

Though the cost of following Christ is high, we do it out of love. God's love should so deeply grip us that we freely choose to live for Him.

Abraham Lincoln once saw in a slave market a young girl for sale. That girl touched his heart. He purchased her and signed paperwork which granted her complete freedom. Lincoln told her, "You are now free. You are no longer a slave!"

She looked at Mr. Lincoln and asked, "Am I free—free to go anywhere I like?"

Lincoln said, "Indeed you are!"

"Then, master," she said, "I will follow you forever."[5]

A life devoted to Christ brings consequences. We give ourselves over to God who does a little whittling. He desires to shape us into something beautiful. It's still us, just minus all the extra stuff we think we need to look good, to feel safe, or to be loved.

God desires to whittle that part of us away. At times, His whittling hurts. Christ intends to shape us into humble, pure-hearted, and loving disciples. Jesus desires dedicated disciples who love Him to such an extent, that their love for anything else pales in comparison.

Yes, I do think Jesus likes to whittle.

Entering the Story

Today would cost me. It would cost me valuable time working in our family vineyard. Yet, I simply must go and hear Jesus teach. I hear He is nearby.

I am getting more and more intrigued by the Rabbi Jesus. His teachings are powerful. His healings are undeniable. His character is irrefutably good. I was initially skeptical, for I knew Jesus as a boy. That's right. We grew up in the same village. His father was a carpenter. My dad owned a vineyard. We often played together as young boys. As the custom, we learned the trade of our fathers. Jesus became a carpenter. I learned to run our family vineyard.

Our vineyard is small, but we are intensely proud of our grapes and wine. Thieves often try and snatch our precious grapes. It became prevalent enough that we commissioned Joseph and Jesus to build us a fence surrounding our vineyard and a watchtower. They worked up a design, drawn on parchment, and informed us of the cost.

It would take all the money we had and then some. My father felt desperate enough to give them the go ahead. "We must put an end to it," Dad blurted out! After the foundation and the first of the timbers were erected, we ran out of money. Construction stopped and the ridicule began.

We often heard, "Quick to start, but slow to finish!" Or folks would say, "Thanks for giving our village that eyesore!" Man, that got old. Luckily, we had a great harvest that year, and we were able to complete the tower. It was fantastic to have it done. The stealing stopped, and so did all the ridicule.

Years later, Jesus became a rabbi. His fame grew. And I could not help myself; I had to go hear Him speak. *What was Jesus like now as a rabbi?* I wondered. The day I went to hear Him, it seems half of Galilee did as well. I could not believe the size of the crowd for my childhood friend!

Jesus seemed troubled that such a great number of people were there. He taught that to follow Him would come at a remarkably high cost. Jesus said that His disciples would need to love Him more than even father or mother! These were strong words. Especially coming from Jesus, who I knew deeply loved His mother and father.

He said we must take up our cross to follow Him! We have all seen enough Roman executions to know what Jesus was talking about. Wow, this childhood friend of mine has turned into one tough rabbi!

Then Jesus told a few stories. His first story made me shudder. He asked, "Who would build a tower and not be able to complete it?" He looked at me and gave me a wink. Some in the crowd who knew our story quietly chuckled. I was a little embarrassed, yet the tone of His voice and the way He looked at me showed nothing but love. His face seemed to say, I love you My friend. We have all made mistakes.

I caught up to Jesus afterward, and we talked. Jesus was so kind and compassionate. He said, "Thanks for coming today. I love you so much. I did not mean to embarrass you. Didn't we have such fun as boys? I loved you then, and I love you now. Please follow Me now as a disciple. Yet, you need to know, it will cost you. The Romans are getting suspicious. The religious leaders will soon tire of My message, and the fickle crowd won't last."

Jesus continued, "Just like you were ridiculed when you couldn't complete the tower, I will be ridiculed, mocked and worse yet, beaten and killed."

Jesus continued, "That's right My friend. I will soon die. But My death will be for all. Can you follow Me? I would love it if you would."

Indeed, my old friend was now quite a rabbi. I fell in love with the Rabbi Jesus that day! Jesus, who once erected timbers on our land, would soon be nailed to Roman timbers—

Point of the Parable:

A life with Christ may cost you everything. A life without him isn't worth a thing.

Jesus wants serious disciples; the give-it-all, loyal-to-the-core type.

Jesus said, "Let go of it all and follow Me."

Who would sign up for such a sacrificial life? Only those deeply in love with their Savior!

for the crime of loving too much. It does indeed sound like following Jesus is costly.

Living the Story

Enter time with God with a humble and honest invitation for God to speak to you. Enter as an open book before Him.

- Imagine yourself in the setting of the parable. Imagine every part of the scene. What are your emotions as He speaks?
- God may invite you to give up something in order to love Him more. Ask Him to show you what that might be.
- Is becoming more intimate with God something you truly desire? Are you willing to pay the cost for this intimacy?

A Blessing for You on Your Journey of Surrender

May you know that Jesus is so fond of you that He gave up everything—for you. Jesus even battled and defeated death for you. Jesus lived and modelled complete surrender of His wishes, for the will of His Father.

May you see Jesus on the cross with caring and compassionate eyes. His immeasurable love led Him to that cross.

In response to His love, may you desire to surrender your self-centeredness, your inflated ego—the things that limit and mask the real you. May you give all you have, all you desire, and all your essence into the nail-pierced, open hands of Jesus.

May you be satisfied with only God's love. His love for you already cost Him everything, so there is no need to try and earn it. There is absolutely nothing you need to do to earn His love!

15

Lost and Found

The true adventurer goes forth aimless and uncalculating to meet and greet unknown fate. A fine example was the Prodigal Son—when he started back home.

—O. *Henry*

Then Jesus told them this parable: "Suppose one of you has a hundred sheep and loses one of them. Doesn't he leave the ninety-nine in the open country and go after the lost sheep until he finds it? And when he finds it, he joyfully puts it on his shoulders and goes home. Then he calls his friends and neighbors together and says, 'Rejoice with me; I have found my lost sheep.' I tell you that in the same way there will be more rejoicing in heaven over one sinner who repents than over ninety-nine righteous persons who do not need to repent.

"Or suppose a woman has ten silver coins and loses one. Doesn't she light a lamp, sweep the house and search carefully until she finds it? And when she finds it, she calls her friends and neighbors together and says, 'Rejoice with me; I have found my lost coin.' In the same way, I tell you, there is rejoicing in the presence of the angels of God over one sinner who repents."

Jesus continued: "There was a man who had two sons. The younger one said to his father, 'Father, give me my share of the estate.' So, he divided his property between them. Not long after that, the younger son got together all he had, set off for a distant country and there squandered his wealth in wild living. After he had spent everything, there was a severe famine in that whole country, and he began to be in need. So, he went and hired himself out to a citizen of that country, who sent him to his fields to feed pigs. He longed to fill his stomach with the pods that the pigs were eating, but no one gave him anything. When he came to his senses, he said, 'How many of my father's hired servants have food to spare, and here I am starving to death! I will set out and go back to my father and say to him: "Father, I have sinned against heaven and against you. I am no longer worthy to be called your son; make me like one of your hired servants."' So, he got up and went to his father.

"But while he was still a long way off, his father saw him and was filled with compassion for him; he ran to his son, threw his arms around him and kissed him. The son said to him, 'Father, I have sinned against heaven and against you. I am no longer worthy to be called your son.' But the father said to his servants, 'Quick! Bring the best robe and put it on him. Put a ring on his finger and sandals on his feet. Bring the fattened calf and kill it. Let's have a feast and celebrate. For this son of mine was dead and is alive again; he was lost and is found.' So, they began to celebrate.

"Meanwhile, the older son was in the field. When he came near the house, he heard music and dancing. So, he called one of the servants and asked him what was going on. 'Your brother has come,' he replied, 'and your father has killed the fattened calf because he has him back safe and sound.'

"The older brother became angry and refused to go in. So, his father went out and pleaded with him. But he answered his father, 'Look! All these years I've been slaving for you and never disobeyed your orders. Yet you never gave me even a young goat so I could celebrate with my friends. But when this son of yours who has squandered your property with prostitutes comes home, you kill the fattened calf for him!' 'My son,' the father said, 'you are always with me, and everything I have is yours. But we had to celebrate and be glad, because this brother of yours was dead and is alive again; he was lost and is found'" (Luke 15:4–32).

Listening to the Story

"Honey, have you seen my hat?" That is often my morning battle cry. If it isn't my hat, it's my keys, or my coat. I am forever losing stuff. My sweet wife is my savior, often knowing right where I put things. If not, I go into an all-out search. I tear the house apart until I find it! I can relate to these parables.

Jesus tells three separate stories of finding something quite special that was lost. And each story ends in a celebration. The first story begins with, "Suppose one of you…" The second, "Suppose a woman…" Jesus invites us to imagine losing something valuable. He wants us to feel the emotion of losing something extremely important and then feeling the joy of recovering it.

The people doing the misplacing vary. There is a child (shepherds were often young), a woman, and a father. The value of the loss increases with each story. First, it was one-hundredth, then a tenth, then half. First a sheep, then a valuable coin, then a priceless son. How do you put a value on a lost son? Jesus intended to reach varying tastes, genders, and interests—designed to draw us all into the narrative of lost and found.

Jesus was verbally attacked (once again) for hanging out with folks who, in their view, were nothing short of scumbags. That is the setup to these parables (Luke 15:1–2). So, Jesus wanted to explain why these people (tax collectors and sinners) were attracted to Him and why He enjoyed their company. Let's first consider some of the distinctives of each story.

A Lost Sheep. One sheep out of a hundred strays away and is lost. We cannot read over that too fast. It might seem remarkable that a single missing sheep out of a hundred is even noticed and worth a hunt! To our non-shepherd ears, we might question the wisdom of leaving ninety-nine valuable sheep alone. But to Jesus and His original listeners the response was, "Yes, I'd do the same!" Let's see why.

An individual shepherd would gather his flock each night into an enclosure with a single entrance. The shepherd would call his flock and as they entered one by one, he would count, "…97, 98, 99, wait, I'm one short!" If so, he would block the entrance for the safety of his flock and go after his missing one.[1]

Yet, shepherds often didn't work in isolation. Villages would often have community flocks, with several shepherds teaming up. If an individual shepherd needed to leave, the other shepherds would keep watch over the total herd. The entire village may be aware that a shepherd was on a hunt. On his return with the missing sheep, his "friends and neighbors" within the village would join in the celebration![2] The original listeners may have recalled with delight when this very thing happened to them.

Some interpreters emphasize the idea that shepherds were considered lowly and even outcasts. Yet, let's not forget that Moses was a shepherd, David started out as a shepherd, Rachel tended sheep, and Jesus presented Himself as the Good Shepherd who lays down His life for His sheep (John 10:11). And David, penning Psalms 23, depicted God as our shepherd.[3] Even if a shepherd held a relatively low position in society—Jesus asks His audience to picture themselves as one! (This was perhaps to make the Pharisees feel more than a little uncomfortable.)

Is Jesus inviting us to be the shepherd who cares enough for each sheep that we go after one as though it were our only one? Or are we to see God as the loving Shepherd, always finding us when we go astray? Hold onto those thoughts as we consider the other two parables.

A Lost Coin. Our next person on a hunt is a gal who misplaces a coin. What strikes me is she seems to be a stand-alone, take-care-of-herself, knows-what-she-is-doing gal. I like that! She seems to have her own home and her own group of friends. A husband is at least never mentioned.

The silver coin was a drachma, roughly a day's wage. But the coin was extremely more valuable than that to this woman. Hebrew girls would patiently save money until they had 10 silver coins. They would string the coins together and wear them as either a necklace or a headband (Semadi). It was her own property, hers and hers alone, never to be taken, even to settle a debt.[4]

The Semadi worn by every matron of the family was a treasured heirloom, often passed on from mother to daughter.[5] A similar custom can be found across the Middle East, varying slightly from region and tribe. Bedouin women from the Sinai wear scarves with silver coins sewn onto the fabric. Even modern Arab women love to wear gold or silver bangle bracelets. And they hold special significance. The jewelry today, as in older times, is hers and hers alone, and often serves as her emergency fund.

With this context, it is much easier to understand how she would fret over the loss of a single coin. It was much more than a simple coin. It was much more than a tenth. It represented her security, signified her womanhood, and gave her the respect a matriarch deserves. The coins were indeed quite special.

Jesus gives us a vivid and clear picture of the search. She lights a lamp. She sweeps the floor. She does not wait until the daylight of tomorrow. She rummages through her probable dirt and dried-reed floor with the dim light of an oil lamp. She does not rest until she finds it. The search may even keep her family awake. And when she finds her treasure, it's time to party with friends!

We are to feel her delight as she re-strands her Semadi with all ten coins and gleefully celebrates! The coin is part of her treasure, once lost and now found. And her friends, willing to celebrate with her late into the night, are a treasure as well.

If the person doing the losing and searching in each story represents God—then we need to realize that in this parable, God is represented as a woman. And if this makes you uncomfortable, you may sit with that awhile and ask yourself why. Oh, the power of a story to break our stereotypes!

Or, if you felt especially drawn to the woman, then you may want to reflect on your own feelings of loss. What have you lost out on in life? What do you desperately want to find?

A Lost Son. Jesus continues with yet another parable, perhaps, the most celebrated parable of them all. This time it isn't an absent-minded person doing the losing; it's a misguided son who himself wants to be lost! This is a son in search of an adventure on his own terms, to live on the edge, even if it means losing it all. No need to sugarcoat this; this son is a spoiled kid who only appreciates what his family provided him once he squanders it.

"There was a man who had two sons." This introduction would be extremely familiar. It's a common storyline to the Jews. Adam had two sons; the younger Abel was favored over his older brother. Abraham had two sons; the younger Isaac is preferred and receives the inherited position of honor. Isaac had two sons, and the younger tricks his father into receiving the primary blessing. David is the youngest of seven and is the special one. Solomon is the second child and is the one to become king. A pattern occurred in their tradition where the younger is somehow special, the beneficiary of God's blessing, and gets the better end of the deal.

So, this second-son-the-special-one pattern, may have come to mind when Jesus began with, "A man had two sons." In this case, the audience would be surprised that the second son is a bit of a brat—an irresponsible and disrespectful kid you'd rather not be around.[6] He wasn't deserving enough to receive a special inheritance, yet he asked for it, even demanded it, and then squandered it! "How dare he?" would be the natural reaction from the crowd! The crowd would be expecting understandably harsh treatment from the father.

In our culture, the thought of a son asking for his portion of an inheritance before his father dies seems cruel. Yet, in Jesus' day, it was not totally uncommon for a man to split up his assets prior to death, if he wished to do so. With two sons, he would normally give two-thirds to the oldest and one-third to the youngest (Deut. 21:17).

This second son has no problem asking for his share to be liquidated so he could fly the coop. What's alarming is what he did with it. His goal was not to own his own farm or business. He headed off to a faraway land and ended up working on a pig farm. This would have told the audience he was in non-Jewish land. The Mishnah states that no Jew may raise pigs anywhere. So, it seems the boy wandered away from his family, his tribe, and his heritage. He wanted things his way.

The son "squandered his wealth in wild living" (verse 13). We do not know what he did. Jesus left that to our imagination. He ended up hungry and desperate, longing for what he ran from. He knew that his dad's hired hands lived better, so he decided to return home and beg for forgiveness.

Theologians debate over whether his contrition was sincere or not. It didn't really matter to the father, did it? What did matter and what we should marvel at, was the love and forgiveness of his dad! Before the son even made it into the driveway, he was greeted and loved on. Before the son can give his rehearsed speech, the father showered him with symbols of honor, restoration, and forgiveness—a ring, a robe, shoes, and a party.

The father loved before there was proof the son deserved it. And that is the shocker of the story. He simply loved. The word prodigal is found nowhere in the passage—it's simply a title given to the story. The son was prodigal because the word means reckless, wasteful, or extravagant spending. The son certainly lived up to the description. So did his father. The father was reckless and extravagant in forgiveness and love!

Remember why Jesus told these stories in the first place? Jesus told of extravagant love in response to complaints about His companions. That is important to see. It's as though Jesus was saying, "Are you really bent out of shape because I enjoy people not as with-it as you? Well then, here is a story for you!"

Here is a story of a father who loves a son who just trashed his own family name and honor. Here is a story of a father who honors that delinquent, unappreciative kid right back with a robe! Imagine a wayward son, who planned on begging to get a job as a hired hand to somehow earn the love of his father back. Instead, that father places a special ring on his finger, signifying he will have a leadership position again!

Servants often didn't wear sandals. They could not afford them. Sons wore sandals. The father slapped sandals on his feet to show the world, "This is my son!"

This is a father who extravagantly loved an undeserving son! It was as if Jesus was saying, "Yes, I accept these sinners. If I had extra sandals, owned a special ring and robe; I would even put those on them, because that's how much I love them!"

And the father's extravagant love did not stop with the returning son. His reckless love extended to his older son as well. The son who never left and who always did everything right. The son who always felt a sense of obligation to honor his father, yet seemingly resented it. This older son cannot stomach going to a celebration for his screw-up, little brother! The father said to the older, rather self-righteous kid, "All that is mine is yours."[7] That is also love.

The Message. So, what is the message of these three lost-and-found parables? I believe we are to appreciate the plight of loss. We are to ponder what we may have lost, whether it's external or deep down in our souls. We may not even realize something is missing. Or we may desperately be aware of our loss.

Maybe you have lost joy in the little things. Perhaps you have lost contentment in who you are. Maybe you've lost the ability to appreciate others. Perhaps you yourself feel a little lost. You may have most everything you ever wanted, yet there is still an empty feeling you can't quite shake.

Perhaps you feel like the screw-up little brother. Then, you need to see that your relationship with God has nothing to do with how well you do! Instead, it has everything to do with His outrageous love! God is always on a love-hunt for you, to bring you home, and to throw a party!

Jesus told the story of the prodigal son to make a simple point: never mind what you've done. Just come home. —Glen Fitzjerrell

No matter what you have done or how you feel, go home. Dive into the loving embrace of God. He always welcomes you back. God loves you no matter which brother you relate to. He loves you no matter what you have thought, said, or done. And He loves you even if you outwardly are doing all the right things, yet inwardly judge all the other "screw-ups" around you.

Speaking of something lost, I went a few days before finding my favorite winter beanie. We finally found it buried in the bottom of the dryer under a mound of socks. You would have thought I found a gold ring of my own. My heart was a little happier. I got a skip back in my step. Life was a little more fun. I felt like I was home.

Entering the Story

As the mother of Jesus, I have experienced loss. That's for sure. I didn't have a typical wedding. We were forced to move around a lot in our early married life. Saying yes to Gabriel so long ago and raising my dear Jesus meant losing out on a normal life.

It's been remarkable to see my own Son grow up into this Galilean Rabbi everyone seems to want to hear. I often ponder the words from that angel that my Jesus would someday be a King. Rabbis from Galilee do not become kings.

Today would be special. I will spend the day with my son. I was immediately gripped by the size of the crowd. People from all walks of life: religious elite, fishermen, venders, farmers, shepherds, tentmakers, carpenters, and even tax collectors were there. Apparently, my son is popular!

What pricked my interest was the sight of the tax men. They seemed to come from every village and appeared to genuinely love my Jesus. I guess it makes sense. Hated by all, Jesus gladly welcomes them and even selected one as a disciple. This infuriates the Pharisees. In their view the Torah clearly teaches not to walk, stand, or sit with sinners. And here, Jesus gladly embraces them!

"How could a rabbi or prophet, as some proclaim Him to be, so blatantly disregard our laws?" they questioned. Jesus could not help but hear their more-than-subtle grumblings, and so He directly looked their way and told a few stories.

"Imagine if you were a shepherd with a hundred sheep. You lose one. Wouldn't you go after the one lost?" Jesus asked. How clever of Jesus. Tending sheep would be beneath a Pharisee, and many of them were clearly insulted. Yet for those still listening, they easily agreed that any worthy shepherd would do just such an act. One even muttered, "God is my shepherd. I lack nothing and, yes, God would find me," as if proudly solving Jesus' riddle.

To my surprise, Jesus then glanced at me. I was sitting with a group of women from our village flanked by Jesus' chosen disciples. Jesus continued, "Or which of you women, if you lost one of your special ten silver drachmas, wouldn't scour the house looking for it?" My friends and I giggled as we remembered a time when I did just that.

How I remember that night. "Jesus, light a lamp," I screamed out when I realized that my strand of coins had come undone! My friends smiled as we recalled my excitement at finding my lost coin. I felt a little embarrassed but honored that Jesus would include me in a story.

Jesus then told a story of a lost son. I must admit, I did not hear much of it. You see, as I looked on with a mother's pride, how everyone hung onto my Son's every word, my mind wondered elsewhere.

My mind took me to the time when I did just that—lost my own precious boy! I lost Jesus for three days in the overcrowded, city of Jerusalem. We had traveled with our family and friends from Nazareth for Passover. After a day's journey, I realized my Jesus was missing. I panicked! Joseph and I searched everywhere in the caravan but to no avail. So, Joseph and I ventured back to Jerusalem.

"Joseph, walk faster!" I exclaimed. Joseph would calmly say, "Mary, saying that every five minutes won't get us there any quicker! We will find Jesus."

It was a horrifying three days of searching in the crowded city. At every corner, I noticed nasty, evil-looking men. I was so scared. It was common for innocent boys to be snatched up and sold into slavery. My heart feared the worst for my special boy, Jesus.

What joy we felt, when we finally found our boy sitting with a group of teachers in the temple. Jesus was engaging in a healthy discussion of the Torah. They were all amazed. I wasn't. I was angrier than a hornet! I let Jesus know how frightened and worried I had been. I'll never forget His words. "Mother, you should have known to go straight to My Father's house."

I've often wondered about those words.

Jesus at that young age, taught the teachers. And here I am seeing it again. My lost son is found. He is teaching us all about what God is genuinely like. He is teaching everyone that God will always search for us. As a shepherd looks for a lost sheep, God will find us. As I looked until I found my lost coin, God will find us. And just as I scoured an entire city until I found my boy, God will find us! God's love is big enough to reach everyone. God will find every last one of us! Yes, I have experienced loss in my life as the mother of Jesus. Yet, this day I am seeing my Jesus in a new and exciting way. He is truly ushering in a new kingdom—one of unbridled love for every soul. My Jesus absolutely loves everyone, much to the dismay of the Pharisees.

Maybe this is what the angel meant by Jesus becoming a king! His kingdom is one of love and acceptance for all.

Living the Story

Put yourself into the scene. Imagine the Pharisees giving Jesus a hard time for hanging out with you! That's right, you! Then imagine Jesus telling these stories with you in mind.

- Which parable most resonates with you? Linger with that parable. How would Jesus speak it just for you?

- What have you "lost" in your life? What do you need to reclaim? Is it the joy of your innocent, inner child? Have you lost contentment in who you are? Have you forgotten that God is crazy in love with you? Have you lost contact with a special someone?

136

- Do you feel lost in any way? Hear God telling you, "No matter what you've done, just come home." How does that make you feel? Journal ways you may need to come home. God will always and forever accept you just as you are now. Do you believe that? Spend time with Jeremiah 31:3.

Point of the Parable:
God always and forever welcomes you home.

Losing something special is annoying. Losing someone special is tragic. At times we ourselves feel lost.

Jesus said, "Come home and I'll throw you a party."

It's time to go home.

A Blessing for You, on Your Return Home

May you know God's extravagant and undeserved admiration for you. God is so proud of who you are, right at this moment. There is nothing you need to do and no one you need to become, to receive his acceptance. You are right now His beloved child.

May you be honest with whatever feels lost in your life. Let God know about your feelings of loss. Allow Him to heal, to restore, and to renew your heart. May you return home and enjoy His embrace.

May you feel His love as you put on your ring, lace up your sandals, and slide your arms into the beautiful robe He has for you. Enjoy the party. It's for you.

16

Being Shrewd

A man without cunning is like an empty matchbox.
—Arab proverb

Jesus told his disciples: "There was a rich man whose manager was accused of wasting his possessions. So, he called him in and asked him, 'What is this I hear about you? Give an account of your management because you cannot be manager any longer.'

"The manager said to himself, 'What shall I do now? My master is taking away my job. I'm not strong enough to dig and I'm ashamed to beg. I know what I'll do, so that, when I lose my job here, people will welcome me into their houses.'

"So, he called in each one of his master's debtors. He asked the first, 'How much do you owe my master?' 'Nine hundred gallons of olive oil,' he replied. The manager told him, 'Take your bill, sit down quickly, and make it four hundred and fifty.' Then he asked the second, 'And how much do you owe?' 'A thousand bushels of wheat,' he replied. He told him, 'Take your bill and make it eight hundred.'

"The master commended the dishonest manager because he had acted shrewdly. 'For the people of this world are

more shrewd in dealing with their own kind than are the people of the light. I tell you, use worldly wealth to gain friends for yourselves, so that when it is gone, you will be welcomed into eternal dwellings'" (Luke 16:1–9).

Listening to the Story

Being a landlord is not easy. The worst part by a mile is when it's necessary to evict someone. I think I would rather get a tooth pulled without pain killers.

God has a great sense of humor. The week I was pondering this parable, the sheriff called and said, "Wednesday at 2:30. That's when it's going to happen. And be sure not to tell the tenant the day and the time…for our protection."

I kind of shuddered and my heart skipped a few beats. After many weeks of running paperwork through the court system, obtaining a favorable ruling from the judge, and delivering three notices to the tenant to please pay or evacuate the premises, it all came down to…Wednesday at 2:30. That is when we would knock on the door and remove all their belongings if they hadn't already. Wednesday came. They hadn't. So, we did.

It was excruciatingly hard. Even though the law was on our side, as in a sheriff literally standing next to me, I still felt horrible. People in the business tell me I will get used to it. I doubt it.

And here we have this parable, where an owner learns the manager of all his affairs is floundering or skimming profits. The owner brings him in and states, "What is this I hear? Bring in the books so I can see for myself. And by the way, you're out of here!" The less-than-reputable manager was soon to be out a job and his livelihood. Indeed, I could relate to the owner's position.

Let's take a look at our two characters in the story.

The Shrewd Manager. This guy was caught red-handed with little to say for himself. He had no defense. So, he sought advice from his favorite person, himself. Being a master manipulator of the books, he concocted an ingenious plan to gain a few friends for a beneficial payback in the future.

He seemed to excel at deceit, whether it was devising lies or listening to them. *I am not strong enough for manual labor,* he thought. *I am too proud to beg,* he concedes. He knew that once word of his antics got out, no other landowner would ever hire him again. He was in a pickle.

But is it true that he couldn't do anything to support himself? I kind of doubt starvation was his only option. But lies always breed more lies. So, he lied and cheated again to win some favors.

The rope of a lie is short. —Arab Proverb

In the first century, it was common for rich landowners to hand the reins of their business to a manager. Think of Joseph managing the business affairs for Potiphar. Potiphar "left all that he had in Joseph's charge" (Gen. 39:6).[1] More than likely, the landowner contracted the manager to oversee the farming of his property, and they would split the profits. In Jewish law, the manager had complete control over the business.[2] So, having an honest manager was critical.

The shrewd manager was making use of another cultural norm that may slip past our modern ears. Generous favors were expected to be repaid. The debtors in Jesus' parable who took part in his maneuvering knew they would be required to repay the odious character down the road.

Finally, the amount of debt reduced (450 gallons of oil and 200 bushels of wheat) was huge, in the range of 500 denarii, or about two years wages for a day laborer.[3] This was some serious cash. It's implied in the parable that he met with many other debtors as well, besides the two mentioned.

The Interesting Landowner. And here is the shocker in the story. The landowner commended the manager for his shrewdness. That's right, he told him that he did brilliant work! I sure wish we could hear how Jesus told the story. These words could have been dripping with sarcasm. As if to say—did you really think that he would get away with it?

I believe this part in the parable was intended to do just that—shock us. The parables can lose their original shock factor because we've either heard them so often or we don't understand the culture behind the story. This one is different. The shock in this story kind of slaps us across the face. We cannot miss it! We cannot help but shake our heads in disbelief. Did Jesus just encourage us to be a knucklehead?

It helps to realize that these metaphorical words within the story are not instructions from Jesus. Jesus had some fun here. He was not commending the crime, or the manager who devised it, but Jesus was complementing his ingenuity. Jesus went on to say that people of the world are smarter with money than perhaps His followers are. Using worldly wealth for heavenly gain seems to be at least part of the message of this story.

Money Matters. It was as if Jesus were saying, if even a scoundrel knows how to be skillful with money, why aren't we? Jesus was not afraid to discuss money. Often, we are. We tend to take one of three different views on money. We either hate it, crave it, or we are clever with it.[4]

We can *hate* it by treating it like a necessary evil. Some Christians feel guilty if they have more than they need, gleaned from such scripture as, "It's easier for a camel to go through the eye of a needle than for someone who is rich to enter the kingdom of God" (Matt. 19:24). And we wonder if Jesus had a sense of humor. Just try imagining a camel with their hideously long and awkward legs attempting to fit through a small hole! You end up with a smile.

Have you ever wondered why Jesus waited until he was 30 years old before he started his ministry? Many scholars believe Joseph died young. He is never mentioned after Jesus is around 12 years old. Jesus more than likely carried on the family carpentry business (along with his rabbinical studies) for several years to provide for His family. Legend has it that Jesus made the best ox yokes in all of Galilee.[5] I like that. Jesus did not have an issue with learning a trade and earning money to care for His family. In fact, a rabbi was expected to have a trade. It was not a paying gig.

The other extreme is we can *crave* money. We can be a slave to it. We can pour all our energy, time, and effort into earning more and more, not knowing when enough is enough. The result might be that we indeed gain riches but at the expense of what's truly more important in life.

Money is a terrible master but an excellent servant.
—P.T. Barnum

Jesus was encouraging a third approach to money—to be *clever* with it. Don't be afraid of it or crave it. Simply, treat it as a friend. By using our money well, we will neither worship it nor despise it, but use it to bring beauty and blessings to our family and others.[6]

But let's be clear of one thing. The manager in the story was a cheat, a knucklehead, and a liar to the core. There is no getting around that. Yet he is credited for maybe the only thing he is good at—he has street smarts. This parable, then, should give us plenty of hope. When we feel like a loser, God loves us just the same. When all we see is our faults, God sees our best. Here is the thing—we can never goof up enough to be outside the love of God!

God is, in fact, shrewd Himself. He forever sees the good in us. God is committed to seeing us grow into wonderfully good people. And it takes some serious skill to make that happen with the likes of us! God is much better at managing me, with all my shortcomings, than I will ever be as a rental-unit manager. That is for sure.

And I will never be evicted from His presence nor His love!

That is a relief. I would not want God to have to go through my underwear drawer!

Entering the Story

With numbers, I rarely make a mistake. The one thing I've always been good at is math. At least that is what I always heard growing up. It's what helped me get the position of tax man.

Yes, I was a collector of taxes for Rome in my hometown of Capernaum. As a result, I was hated by my countrymen. I would like to see them endure what I go through when I am exploited by Roman soldiers and mistreated by my own people. I live with rejection every day.

Part of my job was to keep a meticulous ledger of taxes owed and paid for every family in Capernaum. Rumor has it some collectors skim off extra money for themselves. I would never dream of such a thing, yet many of my former friends assume otherwise. I lived a lonely life.

That all changed the day Jesus asked me to be a disciple. I jumped at the chance! Luckily, the Romans found a replacement, so they agreed to let me go. I love being a part of Jesus' inner circle and having good friends again, although gaining their trust has not been easy.

Today, Jesus told a story of a rich landowner having many acres of fertile farmland. He hired caretakers to farm the land and work the olive grove. He also had a manager to oversee the entire operation and to keep his books.

I can sure relate to this story! I remember shuddering in fear every time the soldiers came to collect. If they suspected I was holding out on them, I was in big trouble. As a result, I was meticulous and honest to the core. I would never cheat someone. The soldiers knew this, and so they trusted me. In Jesus' story, when the landowner confronted the manager, I cringed. I knew how awful that would be. The manager was a scoundrel who devised a way to cheat his master. *What a rat,* I thought! *He deserves what's coming to him!*

But, to my surprise, the master commended him for his cleverness. What? I was appalled! Jesus looked my way and seemed to know exactly what I was thinking.

I could not stop wondering what Jesus meant by this story. I thought about it all day until later that night when I had a chance to ask Jesus about it. "Jesus, I was always honest in my bookkeeping. Why did you tell a story honoring someone who wasn't? I don't get it," I said.

Jesus said, "Let's take a walk. You are a wonderful and honest man. It's why I asked you to follow me. I love you for that! You are nothing like the manager in my story."

Jesus asked, "The manager was a crook, but what was he good at?"

"I suppose he was good at devising a survival plan. He was smart. I give him that," I replied.

"Exactly," said Jesus. "I also want you to use your smarts. Be smart in how you treat others. Remember how you felt when you were hated by your countrymen? I need you to love everyone—not just your new friends. You need to forgive the Galileans who treated you so harshly. Be smart and love well," Jesus said. "I too, was smart when I asked you to follow Me. Because of you, many of the tax collectors are changed men."

"Jesus, I may be smart with numbers, but in many ways, I goof up all the time," I told Jesus.

"I've never noticed," He said.

Jesus continued, "I love you just as you are. God made you with an exact design in mind. And God never makes a mistake."

Living the Story

What do you think of this parable? Be honest. Put yourself in the setting and imagine Jesus telling it.

- Like the manager who felt he could not do anything else to survive but cheat, what lies about yourself do you listen to? Spend solitary time with a listening heart and ask God to show you the lies you entertain in your head.

Point of the Parable:

Be smart. Love well.

The manager in the story was a cheat and a knucklehead. Yet Jesus loved his street smarts.

Jesus said, "Use your earthly brain for heavenly gain."

Nothing will stop God from loving us, not even when we are the knucklehead.

- Like the landowner who commends the shrewdness of the manager, what would Jesus praise in you? What are the things you are exceptionally good at?

- What is your view on money? Journal your thoughts on how you could better use what God has given you. How could you spread the love of God using it?

A Blessing for You,
in Your Honest and Innocent Walk with Jesus

May you know that God sees the best in you. God knows you inside and out, every thought you ever had, and He loves what He sees. He designed all your strengths and gifts, and even allowed for your flaws. All of you is by design. And after He formed you, He said, "You are so good!"

Jesus can empathize with whatever you are going

through. May you be perfectly honest and vulnerable with your struggles and weaknesses. There is no reason for shrewd maneuvering.

May you be true to who you are; you are wonderfully made. May you be the best version of you; wholly human yet Christ-like—gentle and caring.

May you know the immeasurable riches of God's love for you. You can never mess up enough to be outside of God's love. May you know that.

17

Poor Rich Man

If you can't feed a hundred people then just feed one.
—Mother Theresa

There was a rich man who was dressed in purple and fine linen and lived in luxury every day. At his gate was laid a beggar named Lazarus, covered with sores and longing to eat what fell from the rich man's table. Even the dogs came and licked his sores.

The time came when the beggar died, and the angels carried him to Abraham's side. The rich man also died and was buried. In Hades, where he was in torment, he looked up and saw Abraham far away, with Lazarus by his side. So, he called to him, "Father Abraham, have pity on me and send Lazarus to dip the tip of his finger in water and cool my tongue, because I am in agony in this fire."

But Abraham replied, "Son, remember that in your lifetime you received your good things, while Lazarus received bad things, but now he is comforted here, and you are in agony. And besides all this, between us and you a great chasm has been set in place, so that those who want to go from here to you cannot, nor can anyone cross over from there to us."

He answered, "Then I beg you, father, send Lazarus to

my family, for I have five brothers. Let him warn them, so that they will not also come to this place of torment." Abraham replied, "They have Moses and the Prophets; let them listen to them." "No, Father Abraham," he said, "but if someone from the dead goes to them, they will repent." He said to him, "If they do not listen to Moses and the Prophets, they will not be convinced even if someone rises from the dead" (Luke 16:19–31).

Listening to the Story

While living in third-world countries, we were often bombarded by the poor. The poor were seemingly everywhere and hard to ignore—especially when they sat at our own front gate. They needed help and were not afraid to ask for it.

How one deals with a steady stream of desperate people is something you are forced to navigate when living in a poor country or an inner city. And it really doesn't matter what your financial status is. To the impoverished, most everyone else is rich.

As a caring person, it gets difficult sometimes. You want to help, but you cannot help everyone. So, whether planned or not, some people you ignore. That's the predicament of our main character in this parable. The story juxtaposes a man rich beyond compare, with one in desperate need, camped out at his front gate, hoping for any kind of handout.

A Rich Man. Let's look at the subtle clues in the story to get to know our main character. Within the first few words, "There was a rich man…" is our first clue that he is the dubious character.[1]

Jesus commonly voiced his views on the unfair social disparities He saw.

But woe to you who are rich, for you have already received your comfort (Luke 6:24).

Blessed are you who are poor, for yours is the kingdom of God (Luke 6:20).

So, our main character is on the wrong side of the woe-versus-blessed fence.

He also was more than a little well off; he was filthy rich! He was "dressed in purple and fine linen." For us, this may be a peculiar choice of colors; I mean, what dude wears purple? Purple was rare and expensive. Purple dye came from marine snails.[2] You read that right. In ancient Rome, marine snails were gathered up by the thousands and boiled for days in lead vats to produce the costly color.

And what about wearing linen? It sounds more appropriate for bed sheets. Even today, not just anyone wears linen. In the ancient world, the expensive cloth was worn only by the wealthy or perhaps a priest.

He also ate very well. The ESV says he, "feasted sumptuously, every day." I don't know about you, but these word choices sound delicious and make me hungry right now! This guy gorged on the finest cuisine, all the time. The words describe what most people only did at major feasts or festivals.[3] This guy had his fill and then some, *every day*. In the stroke of only one sentence, Jesus masterfully let us know this guy is dripping in money and is not afraid to enjoy it.

It's not just that he liked to dress well and eat often, but he did so while there was a starving and hurting man at his gate. He was downright heartless. He appears to pay no attention to him. Jesus instructed that, "When you give a banquet; invite the poor, the crippled, the lame, the blind, and you will be blessed" (Luke 14:13). This man did not roam the streets looking for needy people to invite to his elaborate meals. Worse yet, he didn't even notice the suffering soul on his doorstep!

Some Jews at the time felt that the rich were well off because of God's blessing and that the poor were somehow getting what they had coming to them because of sin. So, the rich would often intentionally ignore the poor. Yet, this view was flat-out wrong. Hebrew Scripture clearly taught they were to care for the poor.

The generous will themselves be blessed, for they share their food with the poor (Prov. 22:9).

Give generously to them (the poor) and do so without a grudging heart (Deut. 15:10).

As a matter of fact, the Hebrew word for giving alms (*tzedakah*) comes from the same root word for the righteous (*tzedek*).[4] In other words, right living means giving. Our rich man outright ignored the poor man. The original audience would have recognized right away this guy was bad news. Our main character may have been rich, but he was a poor rich man.[5] He was incredibly poor in character. He made poor choices. And he met an unexpected poor fate in the end.

A Poor Man. Lazarus was his name. This is significant for a few reasons. It is so much easier to ignore someone when they remain nameless. This is the only parable where Jesus gives a name to a character. The only one! The very fact that he has a name is extremely noteworthy.

We currently live in a small mountain town. For many years, we only had one homeless man in our little town. One day I referred to him as the "homeless man." Tina, my wife, said "Do you mean Chris?" That jolted me. To me, he was nameless. To Tina, he was Chris. He mattered enough to have a name.

To the rich man in our story, the poor man was simply part of the landscape.[6] Like me with Chris, I doubt if he knew his name.

But the significance of his name gets even better. The name Lazarus means, "whom God helps." Just how clever is Jesus? God was Lazarus' only chance for help. Little-to-no help was coming from the other side of the gate, that's for sure.

Lazarus was in dire straits, not only because he was poor and hungry, as bad as that is. He was covered with sores. Worse yet; his only companions were dogs that lick his wounds. Imagining this scene makes me cringe. Lazarus cannot get a meal, but scavenger dogs turn his wounds into their meal!

Why do I say scavenger dogs? Dogs were simply not kept as pets in Palestine. Puppies were maybe a temporary pet for a child. Yet, dogs were mongrels and despised scavengers.[7] We saw this for ourselves, living in the Middle East, where, even today, most people would never own a dog. So, the point being, dogs licking the sores of Lazarus would have been a further demeaning experience, if not outright frightening.

What's fascinating is dog saliva may have indirectly helped heal Lazarus' wounds. Enzymes and other compounds in dog saliva can kill bacteria and can even act as a mild pain reliever. It's why dogs lick their own wounds.[8] Still, picturing street dogs licking my wounds does not sound inviting.

Lazarus was in a world of hurt and hoping to get table scraps from a man dripping in money. We are to feel his agony. There is no mention that the rich man helped. His only help came when angels carried him into the embrace of Abraham. I use the word embrace because the Greek word (*kolpos*) used in the passage literally meant bosom. I rather like the symbolism of Lazarus getting a warm hug from his hero.

When a needy person stands at your door, God Himself stands at his side. —*Hebrew Proverb*

To be in Abraham's bosom for a Hebrew would be the highest bliss of heaven. The words convey both intimacy and feasting. It's a beautiful picture of a warm cuddle for someone who received very little pampering on earth. It's also a picture of sitting alongside an idol at a banquet table. Lazarus finally got a feast—and he got it with the father of his tribe.[9]

Many people will come from the east and from the west.
These people will sit and eat with Abraham, Isaac, and
Jacob in God's kingdom (Matt. 8:11–12 ERV).

There is a stark contrast with what happened at their deaths. The nameless rich man was honored with an appropriate burial. I imagine lofty words of platitude were spoken. No such words were spoken for Lazarus at his death. Yet, what he did receive was an angelic escort into Abraham's embrace.

The Reversal. The parable describes a rather elaborate reversal of fortunes. Lazarus was now in heavenly bliss. The rich man was in agony. He also saw how nice Lazarus had it. What's baffling is he lacked any hint of remorse for how he treated Lazarus. He was hurting and begged for relief. Yet, he asked for Lazarus to be sent down to ease his agony. And he asked if Lazarus could deliver a message to his brothers. He appeared to still view Lazarus as someone beneath him.

Jewish tradition believed in a heaven and hell within sight of each other. This only added to the misery of hell. A gate separated the two men on earth. In the afterlife, there was an impossible-to-cross chasm keeping the two apart. And they switched sides.

The Message. If this parable of Jesus doesn't pull on your heart strings to help the poor "at your gate," I'm not sure anything will. Do you see the poor around you? Do you know them by name? Do you know their story? Do you feel compassion to help?

When I first sat with this story, I thought to myself, *why doesn't our church do more for the poor in our community?* Then it hit me. *Why don't I? And if I don't; I am the hideous poor rich man.*

The rich man desired a wake-up call for his brothers so that they would do better. This is what the parable should do for us! The only question is if we will heed the warning?[10]

Chris, the homeless man, no longer lives in our little town, but we have plenty of other needy people who do. I am now motivated to learn who they are.

If there is a fundamental challenge within these stories, it is simply to change our lurking suspicion that some lives matter less than others. —Greg Boyle

Entering the Story

I love it when I get to see Jesus. I live a day's walk from Jerusalem. I am training to become a rabbi, which means I shadow my rabbi all day long. My friend and I dream of becoming well-respected teachers someday. For now, we have much to learn.

We have been struck by the new teacher, Jesus. We love it when our rabbi takes us to hear Jesus. It seems like everyone else wants to do the same. Some soak up His every word. Some are skeptical. But nobody can stay away.

The poor and hurting are especially drawn to Jesus. I'll never forget the day I found out why. Jesus was telling stories, which is the tradition of rabbis. He told a startling story of a filthy rich man and a desperately poor man. The poor man's name was Lazarus, or "Who God Helps."

No wonder the poor love Jesus. With a clever mention of his name, Jesus showed that God helps the poor. The rich man, on the other hand, was nameless. That contrast immediately struck me. Because of the rich man's arrogance and disregard for Lazarus, his relationship with God was distant. Lazarus, however, God knew well.

We were convicted to say the least! My friend and I decided then and there, to change our goals in life. We decided to minister to the poor and helpless in our village after becoming rabbis.

A year later, we heard news that Jesus had been unjustly crucified by the Romans. We walked the journey to Jerusalem to see for ourselves. We couldn't believe all that we witnessed over those few days. Some people were saying they spotted Jesus after His crucifixion—that He somehow rose from the grave! His closest disciples were hiding, fearing for their own lives. To say we were bewildered and confused was an understatement. When we spotted Mary Magdalene racing towards the city, we stopped her and asked what was up. "I just spent time with Jesus! Gotta go and tell the boys," she exclaimed.

On our journey home to Emmaus, a man seemed to pop out of nowhere and join our conversation. We were discussing all the news concerning Jesus. We were surprised that this man knew nothing about it. The man then masterfully pointed out all the scriptures that mention that our Messiah must suffer. Why hadn't we put it all together like he had? It all made so much sense now.

My heart burned in excitement—almost like the way my heart burned when Jesus told us that story of Lazarus a year earlier. We were so captivated by this man; we asked him to stay with us in our home. He obliged. My wife had prepared a wonderful meal. We began with some bread and wine. The stranger took the bread and broke it. At that very instant, we knew it was Jesus! We had seen Him break bread like that many times before.

He looked at me with such love. His face communicated approval for who I had become. His eyes said he was pleased with the way we cared for the poor in Emmaus. As suddenly as we realized He was Jesus, however, He vanished! We hated to see him go!

Over the years, I've realized Jesus never really left. For, in every poor and helpless person that we feed, clothe, and care for, we know Jesus is there. We see Jesus in their faces. And to every person I help, I like to whisper, "Lazarus, God loves you! God sees you. God cares for you!"

"I see you, Jesus."

Living the Story

Read and re-read this parable. Soak it up. Imagine Jesus telling it just to you. You may imagine the poor man as someone you have seen in your community. Maybe he is someone that often holds a sign asking for help.

- Is your heart touched by the story? How might you better serve the needy in your community?

- You might imagine yourself to be Lazarus in the story. Imagine the torment you feel everyday as the rich man walks by. Would you be willing to forgive—to deliver water to comfort the rich man from heaven after he constantly neglected you?

- Has the parable encouraged you to care more for the poor? Do you have friends and family that need to be warned?

Point of the Parable:

God helps the helpless. And He wants to use you to do the helping.

The poor and needy are all around. The only question is will we help.

Jesus said, "Have pity on the poor at your front gate."

God sees the poor. God comforts them. Why don't we?

A Blessing for You, to be Rich in Goodness

May you be thankful for the abundance of health, comfort, and good things God has provided for you. May you appreciate God's presence in your life, even in times of despair, need, and discouragement. May you notice how God tangibly loves and cares for you.

May you see with new eyes those around you in need, whether financially or emotionally. May your heart yearn to help. May you pursue justice for the poor and help provide what those around you need.

May you feel the fine linen and know the richness of God's love for you.

18

Relentless for Justice

Justice will not be served until those who are unaffected are as outraged as those who are."
—Benjamin Franklin

Then Jesus told his disciples a parable to show them that they should always pray and not give up. He said: "In a certain town there was a judge who neither feared God nor cared what people thought. And there was a widow in that town who kept coming to him with the plea, 'Grant me justice against my adversary.'

"For some time, he refused. But finally, he said to himself, 'Even though I don't fear God or care what people think, yet because this widow keeps bothering me, I will see that she gets justice, so that she won't eventually come and attack me!'

And the Lord said, "Listen to what the unjust judge says. And will not God bring about justice for his chosen ones, who cry out to him day and night? Will he keep putting them off? I tell you; he will see that they get justice, and quickly. However, when the Son of Man comes, will he find faith on the earth?" (Luke 18:1–8)

Listening to the Story

This is an interesting parable. Luke introduces it and seemingly solves the riddle before it even begins. Everyone knows when telling a story or joke, you do not give away the punch line. So, that is more than a little intriguing. Jesus told His story to show His disciples to, "Always pray and to not give up."

The two characters are quite interesting as well. It certainly teaches about being relentless in prayer. Yet, it also speaks to the need for justice. The words justice or unjust appear five times in this super short story, so that must be significant.

The judge is the primary character, being mentioned more than the widow. And Jesus' words in verse six, "Listen to what the unjust judge says," indicate that he should be our focus.

Let's explore both characters.

The Judge. He is described by Jesus as the "unjust judge." This is an oxymoron at its finest. Unjust is the same Greek word (*adikia*) used for the dishonest manager commended for his shrewdness in Luke 16:1–9. He neither feared God nor respected men. And the thing is, he knew it! In the story, he talked to himself and said it. Some judges at the time took bribes. That may be the case for this guy.[1] He was bad news and certainly not a judge you would want to face in court.

A description from an actual historical court hearing from antiquity bears an uncanny resemblance to our parable.

When you entered the ancient city of Nisibis, Mesopotamia (modern Turkey), you first encountered on one side, a prison with barred windows with prisoners thrusting their arms at you, pleading for alms. On the opposite side was an open hall, the Court of Justice. On the far end of the court, half buried in plush cushions sat the judge or Kadi. Around him sat various notables.

People crowded into the open courtyard, crying out for their case to be heard. The affluent litigants whispered to the notables, offering bribes in hopes to gain an edge. No doubt, the order of the hearings corresponded to the size of the bribes.

Meanwhile, a poor woman in the crowd constantly interrupted the proceedings, screaming out for justice. She was sternly told to be quiet. But, for days on end, she persisted. Finally, the judge demanded, "What does the woman want?" It was her chance. She told of how her only son had been taken away to serve in the army. Alone, as a widow, she was unable to work her land, yet she was still being forced to pay her taxes. The judge ruled, "Let her be exempt." Her perseverance was rewarded.[2]

This is an amazing real life, historical parallel to our parable.

Parables were and still are, intended to shake us up a bit. They should help us reconsider our current ways of thinking and patterns of living. They should open our eyes to new possibilities within God's world. They should cause us to align our world with His.

The parable does this by presenting both characters differently than we would presume. Judges were meant to protect justice and to take care of the helpless.

Judge fairly; defend the rights of the poor and needy (Prov. 31:9).

Do not take advantage of the widow (Ex. 22:22).

This judge is not what a judge should be. Judges were to ensure widows were not taken advantage of. The judge was the widows last and only hope and, for a while, he only ignored her.

As in the parables of "Hitting it Big" (rich farmer in 12:17–19), "Being Ready" (unfaithful manager in 12:45), "Lost and Found" (prodigal son in 15:17–18), "Being Shrewd" (dishonest manager in 16:3–4), and "Resisting Change" (vineyard owner in

20:13), our judge had a conversation with himself and, in this case, it brought him to his senses.

The judge thought, *Even though I do not fear God or care about people, yet because this widow keeps bothering me, I will see that she gets justice, so that she won't eventually come and attack me.* Sadly, he did not care about what was right. He only relented because of her constant badgering.

In the Greek, the words "bothering me" (*parecho*) are very strong and literally mean "causing me trouble." The words "attack me" (*hypopiazo*) mean, "to assault" or "to give a black eye."[3] Yet, as valuable as word studies in the Greek are, we must remember this is a story intended to stir our imagination. Did the judge really fear physical violence from the widow? I kind of doubt it.

These words surely are metaphorical or sarcastic. However, he did fear she might annoy him to death.[4] The judge could also be afraid of losing face, which is important in Middle Eastern culture.

The Widow. Widows were easily recognized by their distinctive clothing. That's right. It's bad enough to be a widow, but they had to dress as one! Perhaps this was a way to alert people that they could use help.

She took off her widow's clothes, covered herself with a veil to disguise herself (Gen. 38:14).

She put funeral clothing around her waist and wore widow's clothing (Judith 8:5 CEB).

In Old Testament times, widows were often left with little means of support. If her former husband left property, she did not inherit it, although provision for her should be made. If she remained with her husband's family, she would assume a low, almost servant-like position. If she returned to her maiden family, any money exchanged at the wedding had to be returned. Widows were often victimized and sometimes sold into slavery.[5]

We have a few remarkable widows in the Old Testament, such as Tamar, Naomi, and Ruth. The most notable is Ruth. Ruth was a model of lovingkindness, loyalty, and surrender. After she and her mother-in-law, Naomi, lost their husbands, she accompanied Naomi to what was for her a foreign land, Bethlehem. She worked as a servant, handpicking wheat left behind from the men harvesters, despite the potential danger from them.

Ruth honored Naomi and her somewhat dodgy plan of sleeping at the feet of Boaz to win his love and gain redemption. Boaz indeed bought back Naomi's former land and took Ruth as his wife. Ruth is a beautiful representation of a vulnerable, yet brave, sweet, and loyal person.

By the time of the New Testament, the plight of widows had improved somewhat. Many women owned their own property. When women married, they did not come under the legal authority of husbands, nor was their property necessarily controlled by him. The wedding dowry was to be returned to her if her husband died. Some women owned property independently. Some widows were even wealthy.[6]

Let's consider the story of Judith, just such an independent widow. The apocryphal book of Judith was written just before the New Testament period. Judith was wealthy; "Her husband Manasseh had left her gold and silver, men and women slaves, livestock, and fields; and she maintained the estate" (Judith 8:7 NRSV). Judith's story is extraordinary, not because of her wealth, but because of her remarkable wisdom and bravery. She cut off the head of an opposing general, thereby ensuring the safety of Israel! She is strong, resourceful, and as feisty as they come. Judith is one tough cookie.[7]

My hunch is that the widow in our parable seems to be poor, like Ruth. Yet, in character, she seems a bit like Judith—stubborn and a force to be reckoned with. She would not take no for an answer. She demanded justice! In fact, the Greek word used (*ekdikeo*) for justice in the parable is unusually strong and can carry the meaning of vengeance. She wanted things to be set right; she also wanted the other party to get what they had coming to them!

The Message. Both characters are distinctive. We have an unjust judge. We have a feisty, unrelenting widow. Who are we to relate to? Who are we to see as the God figure? Is there one? If we see the judge as a metaphor for God, we must realize from the get-go that this is a how-much-more-than parable. In other words, if an unjust judge can finally be badgered into giving a helpless widow justice, how much more will our loving God give justice to those who ask.

As such, the parable is a charge for relentless prayer. God surely wants all our hearts. Sometimes, the degree of our desperation determines the level of our passion in prayer.

When my wife, Tina, was diagnosed with stage 3, ovarian cancer it shook our world! Just before her first surgery and months of chemotherapy was to begin, I was trail running and pouring my heart out to God. I was probably more demanding than our widow, pleading to God for healing and medical success. In short, I was desperate and badgering God for help!

God did something special. I heard Him say, *Be quiet and listen!* I was praying at warp speed, and it was as if God had grown tired of my many words. God got my attention and I got quiet. I kept running and quieted my heart to listen. Like young Samuel, I asked God to speak (1 Samuel 3:7–11). After some time, I heard God say, *Rest.* That's right, rest.

I thought, *What? Take a rest from running?* Then, it became wonderfully clear. God was asking me to let go of my fears. Just as I could run on a mountain trail yet listen to His voice of love, He wanted us to accept all that the doctors would ask of us, yet quietly trust Him for success. I could not wait to find Tina. I was so excited! After I told her of my experience, she got a twinkle in her eye and said, "God told me the same exact thing last week!" Tina felt a deep connection to Exodus 14:14, "The Lord will fight for you, you only need to be still."

If the judge is a metaphor for God, we simply must see that God is not like our unjust judge. He is overwhelmingly just, loving, and compassionate. He has our best in mind. He does want all our hearts. And our prayers must be sincere. And sometimes sincerity can only come out of desperation.

But you may personally relate more to the judge and see the widow as representing God. If so, God is the relentless widow, advocating on behalf of the hurting. Perhaps, you are being asked to change, just as the judge had a change of heart! Maybe, your relentless and loving God wants to shake up your priorities a little. He may be asking you to go to bat for those who don't look or act like you.[8]

Never give up on something that you can't go a day without thinking about. —Winston Churchill

Maybe, you are to support the impoverished in your sphere of life. Is this a parable with more than one way to hear it? Is that too big for God? I think not.

Interesting indeed.

Entering the Story

I've been pondering Jesus' words, "The kingdom of heaven is within you" (Luke 17:21) all day. *Just what did Jesus mean,* I wondered.

I feel the love of God the most when I am near Jesus. There is something special about His warmth, His joy, and compassion. I love being with Jesus. So, I am not sure I like the idea of finding His kingdom within me; on my own. I was pondering these words, and my face must have shown it. Jesus asked me, "What are you troubled about?"

I smiled. He was so kind to ask. "I should be caring for you," I said.

He smiled with delight. He said, "Let me tell you a story."

"There was a certain judge, who did not really care about God. He cared even less about the welfare of others."

"What a pitiful judge," I blurted out!

"Exactly," said Jesus. He continued. "There was a widow who had been badly taken advantage of. Her property was taken from her by a man who claimed it was rightfully his. She was left with nothing to provide for her family. Her only hope was to get a favorable ruling from the judge. So, she hounded the judge for days on end. Without bribe money, her case was never heard. Yet, she was persistent. She went to the crowded open court day after day, even though men would aggressively push her into the far corner and glare at her. It was awful.

"She screamed aloud for her case to be heard. She even threatened the judge, interrupting other cases in trial. Finally, the judge succumbed. She was so annoying, and he was beginning to lose face. Some of the men in the crowd snickered at the judge for having no control over the widow. The judge declared, 'Woman, come forward and state your case.'

"She told of her husband's death, and how her land had been stolen. She was desperate and her only option was to sell herself and her children into slavery. You could hear a pin drop in that open courtyard. The judge was touched. He felt compassion, maybe for the first time in his life. He ruled that her land be given back to her.

"He shouted to his clerics, 'Find me the man that took her land and bring him in for trial! He must be punished!' He ordered for two servants to be given to the widow to work her fields. He shouted to the crowd while glaring at the men who had harassed her, 'No one is to harm this dear woman ever again, or you'll have to deal with me!' Suddenly, everyone in that courtyard felt nothing but respect for the judge."

Jesus looked at me and said, "Now, what's troubling you today? Please tell me."

I chuckled. "Jesus, when we are together and sharing our hearts like this, there is nothing in the world that could ever trouble me. I love being with You, Jesus!"

He looked at me with a tender smile and said, "That is exactly what I meant yesterday when I said the kingdom of God is within you. We will always be together, My beloved."

I think I finally understand. There will be a time when Jesus is gone, and I may feel like the helpless widow. Yet, Jesus will always be with me. And I'll never have to fight for His love and understanding, as the widow did. I will always have the ear of God. I never felt closer to Jesus than at that moment. I did not see a judge. I saw in the face of Jesus, my compassionate advocate.

And today, I know Jesus is with me.

Living the Story

Read the passage in a few translations. Ponder the story and let yourself become aware of your feelings. Do you feel compassion for the widow? Do you feel contempt for the judge?

- Journal your thoughts and feelings as you quietly and slowly consider it.

- Journal a memory of when you desperately sought God and He came to you in a special way. Remember that time of answered prayer and feeling His presence.

Point of the Parable:

Be relentless in prayer. Be equally relentless for justice

Sometimes we are desperate for help.

Jesus said, "God will surely hear His beloved when they cry out."

God helps us when we pursue him. God is also in pursuit of us to help the helpless.

- Do you also harbor a memory of when God felt far away? If so, take that memory to Him. Ask God to be near to you now.

- Maybe you relate more to the judge and see God in the widow. What call for justice and compassion is God asking of you? Who can you help and how? Journal what you hear.

A Blessing for You, on Your Quest for Justice

May you feel God's compassion and care, especially if you have been hurt. May you know God sees your tears and He understands. May God shower you with mercy and love.

May you know that God is near, He always listens, as you relentlessly pray to Him. May you quiet your heart. May you listen well. May you feel joy as He speaks peace to you.

May you do more than pray for justice, for prejudice to be gone, and for despair to end—may you be an agent for this work.

May you know you are forever loved by our compassionate King. God is nothing like the unjust judge.

19

Lord, Have Mercy

A great man is always willing to be little.
— *Ralph Waldo Emerson*

To some who were confident of their own righteousness and looked down on everyone else, Jesus told this parable: "Two men went up to the temple to pray, one a Pharisee and the other a tax collector. The Pharisee stood by himself and prayed: 'God, I thank you that I am not like other people—robbers, evildoers, adulterers—or even like this tax collector. I fast twice a week and give a tenth of all I get.'

"But the tax collector stood at a distance. He would not even look up to heaven, but beat his breast and said, 'God, have mercy on me, a sinner.'

"I tell you that this man, rather than the other, went home justified before God. For all those who exalt themselves will be humbled, and those who humble themselves will be exalted" (Luke 18:9–14).

Listening to the Story

When we shop for clothes, we look for the label. The label provides good information about size, price, and type of fabric. Labels on clothes are good, but when we haphazardly label a person, it's not good at all.

Labeling is a subtle but horrible way of placing immediate judgment on someone. "That dude is crazy," we may say. He's a liberal. Millennial. Tree-Hugger. She's a feminist. He's a criminal. He's selfish, lazy, or arrogant. Whether we admit it or not, we all label others to some degree. It's a habit we desperately need to break.

Labeling is horrible because when we do it, we subtly believe that the labelled behavior reflects the person's essence. We assume they will never change. When we think or say, "He's a criminal," we think of him as a criminal for life.

The Pharisee in our parable placed the label, "tax collector," on his brother and mentally put him in a box of hopeless scum. Jesus saw him in a different light. Jesus saw him as a person of value and in need of mercy.

And here is the funny thing. You may have labeled the Pharisee as the nitwit in our story before it even began. It was not the case for the original hearers. To Jesus' audience, he would have started out as the good guy.

This parable may have lost some of its original punch, especially if it is not your first rodeo in reading the Gospels. If you grew up in the church and have heard a sermon or two, you probably view Pharisees as grumbling and pretentious hypocrites, and tax collectors as repentant and receptive to Jesus. Jesus' original audience would have assumed just the opposite.[1]

This is a parable of extreme character contrasts. It also contrasts two ways to pray.

A Pharisee. The name literally means, "separated one." Beginning with the ten commandments, scribes and rabbis amplified the Jewish law until it included tens of thousands of rules—to cover every facet of life. Pharisees were a sect of priests who dedicated their lives to following these rules. They separated themselves from secular activities and ordinary people to help achieve this. This may explain why he stood alone, a safe distance away, to pray at the temple.

Living as a Pharisee sounds extremely rigid to us today. I am not sure any of us would sign up. But when Jesus used a Pharisee in His story, he was using a person of honor in that day.

What is more, this Pharisee goes above and beyond. Fasting twice a week is what some Pharisees commonly did but was way more than required. The Law instructed Jews to fast only on the Day of Atonement. Tithing everything, was also more than typical.[2] They were only required to tithe on certain things. So, the Pharisee in Jesus' story was a cut above—the problem is, he knew it.

A rabbi, named Simeon, once proudly said, "If there are only two righteous men in the world, I and my son are these two; if there is only one, I am he."[3] Talk about confidence in what you believe and how you live! Excuse me while I need to swallow the bit of throw-up in my mouth!

Now, let's look at the Pharisee's posture and his prayer. Standing and looking up while praying was common (see Mark 11:25, Matt. 14:19, and John 11:41). To us today, his prayer might seem a little different and a bit self-centered. God, I thank you…I am not…I fast…I give. That is a lot of focus on oneself. However different to us it seems, this was a common way to pray back then.

From Deut. 26:12–15 (ESV): "When you have finished paying all the tithe…then you shall say before the Lord your God…I have given…I have not transgressed…I have obeyed…I have done what You commanded."

From the Babylonian Talmud, Berakhot 28b: "I give thanks to Thee, O Lord my God; that You have given my lot with those who sit in the seat of learning, and not with those who sit at the street corners; for I am early to work."

From Qumran, 1 QH 15:34–35: "I give You thanks, Lord, because You did not make my lot fall in the congregation of falsehood."

You would stand before God, give thanks, and confess that you have done what God expects. So, the prayer of the Pharisee itself is not where he went wrong. Where he went wrong was to dishonor the tax collector. There was no reason to point out to God that he was better than the low-life (in his eyes) next to him.[4] The Pharisee held a short course on labeling.

I have experienced what it feels like to be looked down on and treated as an infidel (unholy) while living abroad in Muslim countries. One day, I innocently shook a friend's hand when we saw each other in the hallway. The only problem was he had just washed his hands, face, and feet for prayer. He was on his way to the mosque. Much to my surprise, my friend sighed in frustration and marched back in the bathroom to rewash all over again, since he had touched an infidel! I felt belittled. Afterward, we both got a chuckle out of it.

As odd as Pharisees seem, they lived to please God, at least the sincere ones.[5] To put ourselves in the shoes of Jesus' audience, they would have initially viewed him as we might view our favorite pastor or priest. Let's now consider the next character in our story.

A Tax Collector. If the Pharisee was a caricature for being a respected and devout follower of God, the attitude toward the tax collector would be as opposite as one could get. Public opinion equated tax collectors with robbers and murderers.[6] Jesus used as extreme of a contrast as there was.

But why were they so despised? Rome had an interesting way of collecting taxes in their occupied lands. They split up regions, assessed each area a certain tax, and then had locals bid for the job of collecting it. The job went to the highest bidder. The collector would pay the tax plus his bid. Yet, the tax man was free to keep whatever else he collected for himself! This was a system begging for abuse.

And there were plenty of opportunities for extortion because there were a lot of taxes! There was a tax for simply existing (poll tax), a land tax, income tax, an import/export tax, a tax for entering a walled town, sales tax, a road tax, an inheritance tax, and maybe more. That is a lot of taxes! A collector could stop a man anywhere, insist he untie his bundles, and then demand a tax on the spot. If the man could not afford it, the collector might offer to advance him money at an exorbitant interest rate.

What made it horribly worse is that tax collectors were fellow Hebrews. They were traitors to the highest degree—men who sold out to Rome to extort their own people.[7] I am kind of angry right now just imagining what kind of scum would do this!

But the scum in our story is repentant and goes to the temple to seek forgiveness. He stands at a distance, feeling unworthy to even be there. He beats his chest—a symbol for remorse. He looks down because he views himself unworthy to look up to God. And he rightfully calls himself a sinner. In the Greek, he is *the* sinner, as if he considers himself the worst sinner of all. Or maybe he is simply repeating the very words he has heard spoken by others a thousand or so times.[8]

The hated tax collector is displaying true humility. He does not list his good works to God because he doesn't feel he has any. He can only confess his unworthiness. And he prays,

God, have mercy on me, a sinner (Luke 18:13).

It is simple. It is honest. It's beautiful. Turns out, the one thing he does well is pray.

His words form a part of the Eastern Orthodox, Jesus Prayer. Lord Jesus Christ, Son of God, have mercy on me, a sinner. The prayer combines Phil. 2:11 (Jesus Christ is Lord), Luke 1:35 (Son of God), and the prayer of our tax man. What a thought that the prayer from this surprise-of-a-saint tax man has been repeated for over 2000 years by millions. That is quite a legacy. (For an interesting little biography on someone who dedicated himself to the Jesus Prayer; see *The Way of the Pilgrim* by Nina A. Toumanova.)[9]

I must admit. My anger has turned to respect. I love this tax man! I love his honesty and vulnerability. He would make Dr. Brené Brown proud.[10]

And this is the surprising twist in Jesus' story! Jesus states that the tax man is the one who went home justified. What? Those words would have shocked His audience.

Yet, here is the thing. We are not to get caught up in all the wrongs of the Pharisee either. And that just may be the "gotcha" Jesus had in mind for us.

We are not to label the tax man or the Pharisee. We are not to label at all. The essential problem with labeling is it de-humanizes. We put whoever we label into a box of not measuring up...to us! It's actually a subtle way of elevating ourselves!

Lord, have mercy is right!

The Message. The message of this story is that in our mixed-up world, it's often hard to see who the good guy actually is. It's not like in western movies of old, where Hollywood graciously put a white hat on the good cowboy to help us keep track of who's who throughout all the gunfights and chase scenes. We need to once and for all, stop trying to figure out who our bad guy is! We all need forgiveness. We all need God's mercy. Simply put, there is no room for labeling in love.

The point of the parable may simply be that each and every one of us is special, everyone is loved by God to the same degree, and everyone desperately needs to understand that!

Labeling and looking down on others is pathetically wrong, because everyone is a beautiful creation of God. If we look down on others, we look down on God! God honors the truly humble. Sad to say, we tend to exalt the successful and those proud of it!

God, show me where I am too proud. Show me how to be truly humble!

You cannot attain charity except through humility.
—Saint Augustine

We also may need to realize that too often we love going solo. The Pharisee did. He stood by himself. So did the tax collector. He did not think he was worthy enough to stand next to anyone else. We often tackle life on our own because we either do not think others are good enough to join in, or we do not view ourselves as good enough to fit in.

Both the tax collector and the Pharisee must have felt horribly alone. They both needed forgiveness. They share more in common than they realize. The message of the parable may be that we are all more alike than we could ever imagine!

To love is to recognize yourself in another.
—Ekhart Tolle

Maybe it's time we embrace the tax collector's prayer as our own. And no maybe about it; it's time to drop the labelling once and for all.

Entering the Story

God made each of us beautiful and unique. And yet, at the same time, we share so much. We are each on a wonderful journey of transformation and awakening our hearts to God's loving presence in ever-increasing ways.

I have a long way to go myself. Part of my journey has been to learn who I am. I am also learning my default behavioral patterns and how I react to stress.

A tool I have personally found extremely valuable for growth work is the Enneagram. It's been eye-opening. I'm learning there is no reason to stay stuck in my adaptive self using the coping patterns I learned as a child. God invites me to be more authentic to who I am.

So, this is a little about me. I grew up in what I perceived as a scary world. I learned to build a safe environment for myself, where I could feel secure. It sure didn't help losing my mom at the tender age of six and having a critical, harsh father. I grew up afraid of what I might lose next or what my father might say.

So, I learned to power through my fears with grit and determination—an attempt to hide the anxiety I typically felt within. I gained a sense of accomplishment in doing things that might frighten others. Living abroad in sketchy places, in turbulent times, for example.

Yet, I am learning that to power through my fear without recognizing it, is not healthy. Others around me can get caught up in my ugly wake! The healthier approach is to humbly admit my fear and allow God to give me true and gentle courage.

Another thing I have learned to recognize is my tendency for labeling. That's right. It's like this parable was intended just for me! Labeling is my silly way of building what feels like a wall of protection. By labeling a person as some form of—other than me—I can keep them from entering my sphere where they may hurt me.

I also have a hard time trusting people. I sadly enjoy seeing when someone turns out to be a scoundrel. I can say to myself, "I knew it!" I've learned that's not so much a skill in discernment, for I tend to think everyone is a scoundrel at first! Folks must earn my trust. Once they do; I'm a loyal soul for life.

It's been valuable to learn these (and more) default ways of coping and to allow God to change me. I now try to recognize these feelings early as they arise, so as not to be controlled by them.

So, as I sat with this parable, let's just say I could relate. Far too often, I've been the guy, proud of who he is, looking down on the person who doesn't measure up. I've also, often, been too critical of myself, feeling very unworthy of God's love. So, I can relate to both characters.

In quiet reflection, I found myself, crafting my own much-needed prayer: Jesus, help me to see the beauty in those I meet. Help me see it right away, without any labels. Help me rejoice in who they are. Let me notice how they reflect Your love and goodness.

Thank you, God, that you crafted me as you desired. Thank you for even allowing the tragic and hurtful events in my life. They shaped me. They formed me. And besides, You were with me all along. You eased the pain, and You hurt along with me.

Father, may I become increasingly aware of my default behaviors that distract me from You and hurt others. Let me find my security in You alone. Change my heart. Father, I am the sinner. May I see myself fully. May I be the best version of the me You created.

Lord, have mercy on me, the sinner.

Living the Story

Imagine yourself with Jesus when He told this story. Imagine yourself as a Pharisee standing in the crowd. Notice how those in the crowd initially look at you with great respect. But then, how did it feel when you become the punch line in the parable?

Now, imagine yourself as the tax man. Where were you in the crowd? How did others look at you, and how did that make you feel? Then, imagine your emotions as Jesus honored you as the hero in His story.

- Who did you most relate to and why?

- Notice the good parts of the Pharisee's prayer. He does appreciate who God created him to be. Do you? Are you too often too hard on yourself?

- Are you in touch with your body and your emotions when you pray? Can you think of ways to incorporate physical activity with prayer?

• What labels do you tend to use? Try noticing throughout this week who you label. Ask God to show you what hurts might be buried within your heart causing you to label others in this way. Ask God to heal those hurts.

Point of the Parable:

Everyone is special. Everyone needs to see that.

Labeling people is pathetic, for everyone is special to God.

Jesus said, "I will exalt the humble."

The villain in the story prayed, "Have mercy on me a sinner." He was the true hero.

A Blessing for You, the Sinner

May God grant you mercy upon mercy. May you know that God loves who you are! You do not have to become something different, or better, or clean yourself up in any way for God to love you. He just does!

May you be honest and vulnerable before God. May you learn to see your unhealthy habits, whatever they may be. May you cease to label others; except as deeply loved souls, who are fellow sojourners on the road of transformation, growing into the love of God.

May God, who is rich in mercy, invade your here and now. May you become ever-increasingly aware of His presence and His satisfaction of you. You are truly God's treasure!

20

Love over Fear

May your choices reflect your hopes, not your fears.
—Nelson Mandela

While they were listening to this, he went on to tell them a parable, because he was near Jerusalem and the people thought that the kingdom of God was going to appear at once. He said: "A man of noble birth went to a distant country to have himself appointed king and then to return." So, he called ten of his servants and gave them ten minas. "Put this money to work," he said, "until I come back."

But his subjects hated him and sent a delegation after him to say, "We don't want this man to be our king." He was made king, however, and returned home. Then he sent for the servants to whom he had given the money, in order to find out what they had gained with it.

The first one came and said, "Sir, your mina has earned ten more." "Well done, my good servant!" his master replied. "Because you have been trustworthy in a very small matter, take charge of ten cities." The second came and said, "Sir, your mina has earned five more." His master answered, "You take charge of five cities."

Then another servant came and said, "Sir, here is your

mina; I have kept it laid away in a piece of cloth. I was afraid of you, because you are a hard man. You take out what you did not put in and reap what you did not sow." His master replied, "I will judge you by your own words, you wicked servant! You knew, did you, that I am a hard man, taking out what I did not put in, and reaping what I did not sow? Why then didn't you put my money on deposit, so that when I came back, I could have collected it with interest?" Then he said to those standing by, "Take his mina away from him and give it to the one who has ten minas." "Sir," they said, "he already has ten!"

He replied, "I tell you that to everyone who has, more will be given, but as for the one who has nothing, even what they have will be taken away. But those enemies of mine who did not want me to be king over them—bring them here and kill them in front of me" (Luke 19:11–27).

Listening to the Story

Sometimes, life comes down to a simple choice.

Our story is a fascinating parable about choices. Jesus intertwined two narratives into one. There is a prince on a quest to be king. Then, that same nobleman provided money for servants to invest. Will the prince succeed in becoming king? How will the investments go? What will be their reward, if any? How do these intertwined narratives even relate? The story immediately draws you in.

Luke sets the stage. Jesus and his entourage were passing through Jericho on their way to Jerusalem. Most of Jesus' followers were hoping he would become king upon entering Jerusalem—as if Rome would hand over the rule of Judea to a peasant rabbi from the Galilean countryside! I guess one can always hope.

A modern-day, real-life prince made a choice that was rather remarkable. Prince Harry and his wife Meghan willingly gave up their United Kingdom royal status. It is a real-life story full of intrigue. In my view, it is a bit of a love story. Prince Harry, tired of the harsh treatment his wife received from the press, willingly abandoned any chance of becoming king. He chose love over a His Royal Highness title.

Our parable is just the opposite. We have a prince who wants more than anything to become king! And he does whatever it takes to achieve his goal.

If you have heard this parable preached, the message may have sounded like this: We are to be good stewards of all God has entrusted to us—our money, time, talents, and resources. We are to use all we are given to advance the kingdom for Christ. So, go be a good steward, or in the end, you will face an angry God, disappointed in you. I hope that encourages you today!

That feels to me like I've been slapped across the face with a tuna in a seaside fish market. And the God I know and love is not waiting for me to slip up so He can punish me. This is an extremely poor view of God, brought about by projecting a human image of authority onto God. God, in stark contrast, has always loved you and always will love you (Jer. 31:3)!

We are to be good stewards. There is just far more to hear from this marvelous story.

Historical Context. Jesus was a master Storyteller, and His skills are really showcased in this parable. Jesus shrewdly makes use of a real historical event that would have raised eyebrows.

In around 4 BC, Herod the Great died and his kingdom was up for grabs. He ruled for 37 years and was responsible for colossal building projects, including renovating the second Temple, building the mighty fortress of Masada, erecting the Herodian palace, and much more. He had several wives and children, so there was not a clear heir to the throne. Herod chose his son Archelaus to take over the kingdom instead of another son, Antipas. Before Archelaus could become king, however, he had to travel to Rome to gain permission from, none other than, the Roman Emperor Augustus Caesar.

The Jews sent fifty men to Rome to plead with Caesar to not award the kingdom to Archelaus. They were joined by thousands of Hebrews that lived in Rome. I guess he wasn't the people's choice! Augustus heard their case but ruled in Archelaus' favor.

Rome split up Judea into new regions and assigned Archelaus tetrarch (not king) of Judea and Samaria and made Antipas (the Herod who later tried Jesus) ruler of Galilee and Perea. Archelaus ruled an area half of what his father did, was never given the title of king, and his reign only lasted nine years. I guess he didn't work out too well after all.

Josephus details this historical event. He does not specifically record Archelaus killing the fifty men (as in the parable), but states, "Archelaus on taking possession of his ethnarchy, did not forget old feuds, and treated not only the Jews, but even the Samaritans with great brutality."[1,2]

What's more, Herod the Great often resided in Jericho, and he died in this city. Imagine that. Jesus told this story as they traveled through the very city where this real event happened just a few years prior. Yes, Jesus was quite the Storyteller.

The Message. One can draw many lessons from this parable. It certainly teaches we should strive to be good stewards of all the resources God graciously entrusts to us. It is a valuable reminder that God blesses us with so much, and we are to manage those gifts well.

The servants in the parable were given one mina each. A mina was equivalent to 100 drachmas and a sixtieth of a talent. A mina is thought to be worth around 100 days labor. This was not a ton of money, and yet, in the parable of the Lost Coin, the woman tore apart her house in search of a single drachma. So, a mina was certainly significant and enough to invest.

The resources we have been given may feel small. Our talents and gifts may seem insignificant. Yet, God can use them in big ways if we are willing to let Him.

The master in the parable did not expect the same results from each servant. All he asked was that the servants give their best. And he gave each servant freedom to invest as they saw fit. Likewise, God gives us plenty of freedom in our lives. God desires only that we give it our best.

The new king commends the servant who gained ten more—that is a huge return on an investment! And he commends the servant who gained five more. That's a good return as well. The story presents a little downward progression...ten, five, one (at least, one is what was expected). However, the last servant didn't return anything! He only hid it, and the king was greatly disappointed. It was not so much that this servant did not return any gain from his mina, it was that he didn't even try! He played it too safe.

In any given moment, we have two options: to step forward into growth or to step back into safety.
—Abraham Maslow

This servant displayed what is called self-fulfilling prophecy. He was so caught up in the idea that his master might punish him if he failed, that he did fail. Self-fulfilling prophecy is when you think the worse so strongly that you help bring it to fruition. As an example, if enough members of a bank fear a crash and withdraw their money, they can, in fact, cause the bank to crash.

Why would this servant even consider burying the mina? Understanding the historical context will help. An often-quoted Rabbinic teaching commends burying money as a safe way of protecting it (Baba Metzia 42a).[3] Another rabbi from that time said a person should always divide his money into threes, investing a third, burying a third, and using the final third for spending. So, safeguarding money in this manner was viewed as prudent. In fact, Jesus condemning him in His story would have been the surprising zinger!

What caused this servant's play-it-too-safe behavior? Fear. I believe the biggest lesson from this parable is that fear can wreak havoc in our lives. Fear is what underpinned the self-fulfilling prophecy. It crippled him into making the safest, yet poorest choice. The better route would have been to choose love over fear.

We see fear throughout this parable. The citizens hated the nobleman (verse 14) and tried to stop him from becoming king. Hate is typically driven by fear. They feared how miserable life might be under his rule. The servant who buried his mina was so afraid of making a bad investment he didn't make any. And fear also drove the new king to kill the fifty men who opposed him. He was afraid of losing his new kingdom after just gaining it.

Many believe you can reduce all human emotions down to two—love and fear—and that we cannot feel both at once. In the same way that light removes darkness; love removes fear. "Perfect love drives out fear," states 1 John 4:18.

Why is this important? The opportunity to choose love over fear presents itself every day in the big and small moments of life. We choose either love or fear every time someone speaks to us in a hurtful way. We face the choice when things just don't feel right or when life isn't fair. Our choice is how we react—whether in love or in fear.

What does fear look like in relationships? I think we know. When we verbally strike back, or we defend ourselves to prove the other person wrong—those reactions typically stem from fear. It's a survival instinct causing us to retaliate. Our physical survival is not at stake, but our ego is. We want to protect our innocent self.

The better approach is to love. The loving way is to breathe and to listen—without conditions. It's to be courageous enough to try and understand the other person's point of view. It's to open our hearts and to love even when our ego is screaming in fear.[4] That's choosing love over fear.

All healing is essentially a release from fear.
—Helen Schucman

Fear resulted in people making horrible choices in our parable. Fear drove a servant to hide his mina, worked-up citizens to attempt a preemptive coup, and a king to kill. Fear can cause us to act in poor ways as well, or we can freeze and not act at all.

Fear is defeating. Fear can be debilitating.

Love liberates. Fear imprisons. —Gary Zukay

Two servants in the parable made a better choice. They had the same harsh master, soon-to-be king. Yet, they overcame their fear and didn't let it control them. They invested. And they reaped rewards.

Let's choose love over fear in every opportunity we are given.

Let's be a bit like Prince Harry, Duke of Sussex HRH, sixth in line to become King of Britain, who chose not to be a royal. He chose love instead.

Let's choose love.

Entering the Story

It's been a wonderful yet sometimes frightening three years. There were times I warned Jesus to stay away from disease infected people when His heart told Him to heal. There were times I warned against entering cities with crowds plotting to harm Jesus. There were times we all thought we may die at sea. Yes, we have had our fair share of adventures.

Jesus' popularity has now reached epic proportions and there seems to be no stopping Him. Everywhere we go, there are crowds.

I must admit, I miss the secluded times. I miss when the twelve of us would sit around an evening fire with Jesus and talk for hours on end. We would discuss the days' events. Jesus would ask us our thoughts, and we would share our dreams. He cares so much.

He sometimes told stories of His life as a boy, and all that His family went through to keep Him safe. He told stories from His childhood working with His carpenter father and His years as a young apprentice rabbi. These were fun conversations.

Today we are passing through Jericho on our way to Jerusalem. We stop for bananas. Jesus always says the Jericho bananas pop in flavor. (I can personally attest to that!) Then we started our long walk up the steep climb to Jerusalem. I think all of Jericho was following us.

There seems to be anticipation and extra excitement in the crowd. People were wondering if Jesus will take His kingdom soon. You really cannot blame them. Unlike Galilee where we have Herod Antipas, a Jewish ruler, Judea is under direct, brutal Roman rule. They long for a Jewish king.

Jesus sensed their excitement. He could hear the whispers. Suddenly, Jesus stopped walking, and He perched himself up on a large boulder. We all gathered around. Everyone scurried for a seat. We knew what was coming—a story.

Jesus told of a nobleman who traveled far away to seek authority to become king. Yet, there were those who hated him. The crowd was captivated. We all knew he was subtly referring to what happened to Herod Archelaus just thirty years ago. That was the last Jewish ruler Jericho and Judea had.

Jesus certainly had our attention!

Jesus then intertwined a story within the story. The nobleman gave ten servants a mina each and instructed them to invest it. As he told this part, Jesus seemed to look mostly at us disciples.

What would I do with my mina? I wondered. *I guess I could buy a few sheep and try and breed them into a small heard. Or I could buy a small plot of land and grow produce for a nice profit. I could buy my own boat for fishing.* My imagination was swirling. Jesus glanced my way with a loving look.

Then it hit me. Archelaus was incredibly ruthless and if my investment didn't go well, he'd probably sell me off as a slave to recoup his mina! Yes, I knew what the prudent thing to do was! *While the other nine might lose their mina, I would safeguard mine until his return! That would be the wise choice,* I thought. I chuckled when Jesus revealed that the servant who buried his mina made the poorest choice.

Later that day, Jesus walked next to me and asked, "What would you have done with your mina?

"I think You know, Jesus," I said. We laughed. We both knew I was the play-it-safe disciple, always the first to warn Jesus of any danger.

Jesus then tenderly told me, "You need to harness the courage you have. It's there." Jesus continued, saying, "Soon, you will take adventurous journeys of your own, spreading news of me. And you will need to be brave." Jesus then asked, "What frightens you the most?"

"The thought of losing You, Jesus," I said. "I can't bear the thought of something happening to You!"

"You will never lose Me. I will forever be at your side. So, you never need to fear. I will always be with you, to comfort you, and to guide you."

"Can we forever walk together and talk like this?" I asked.

"Always," Jesus said.

Living the Story

Read the parable several times. What strikes you as the main message of the parable? Does it prick your heart to be more loyal, a better steward, or less fearful?

Journal your thoughts.

- Imagine how you would have invested money in Jesus' time. What would you have done with the mina? Have fun with this.

- Are you a play-it-safe person or are you naturally adventurous? How has that played out in your life? Journal your thoughts and thank God for making you as you are.

Point of the Parable:

The surest investment with the highest returns is love.

Fear can be crippling. In our story, it led to poor choices and destruction.

Jesus said, "To everyone who has love, I will give even more."

Our true villain is fear. Only love drives it away. Choose love!

- If you could do anything in your life—anything—what would you do? Why aren't you doing it? Be honest. Is that a good reason to not be chasing that dream?

A Blessing for You, on Your Lifelong Investments

May you know that God has always loved you and that He always will (Jer. 31:3). God is present with you, rejoices over you (Zeph. 3:17), and loves you for who you are right at this moment. God invites you to constantly dwell with Him in love (John 15:9). What a glorious invitation.

May you appreciate what you have and what you aspire to be. May you see them as gifts to be cherished, yet held loosely. May you invest deeply in what is most important.

May you be increasingly more aware of when fear is behind your emotions. May you bravely uncover the talents and aspirations you may have buried long ago. May you explore and reach and jump and play. May you follow your deepest held dreams.

21

Resisting Change

He who rejects change is the architect of decay.
—Harold Wilson

He went on to tell the people this parable: "A man planted a vineyard, rented it to some farmers and went away for a long time. At harvest time he sent a servant to the tenants so they would give him some of the fruit of the vineyard. But the tenants beat him and sent him away empty-handed. He sent another servant, but that one also they beat and treated shamefully and sent away empty-handed. He sent still a third, and they wounded him and threw him out.

"Then the owner of the vineyard said, 'What shall I do? I will send my son, whom I love; perhaps they will respect him.' But when the tenants saw him, they talked the matter over. 'This is the heir,' they said. 'Let's kill him, and the inheritance will be ours.' So, they threw him out of the vineyard and killed him.

"What then will the owner of the vineyard do to them? He will come and kill those tenants and give the vineyard to others." When the people heard this, they said, "God forbid!"

Jesus looked at them and asked, "Then what is the

186

meaning of that which is written: 'The stone the builders rejected has become the cornerstone?' Everyone who falls on that stone will be broken to pieces; anyone on whom the stone falls will be crushed" (Luke 20:9–18).

Listening to the Story

Ducks love water. They rely on water to clean themselves, especially their eyes and nostrils. It is why they submerge their heads. In comparison to other birds, they consume a lot of water. They are designed to float on the surface and their feet are natural paddles. So, yes, ducks enjoy water, although, occasionally, they just don't know it.

A group dedicated to rescuing mistreated animals freed many abused birds. Among them were several ducks who had been restricted to small cages. The cages were barely larger than a single duck. These ducks were in rough shape—hardly able to move, undernourished, and never exposed to life-giving water.

With proper care in their new environment, they soon thrived. Once healthy, the new owners took them to a slow-moving stream where they could do what ducks do—swim and play!

The rescuers were a bit startled. The ducks refused to go in! Never seeing water before, they didn't know what it was. They scampered away every time they were led to the stream. Finally, the owners gently tossed one duck into the stream, and the duck realized how wonderful it was! He splashed about and had the time of his life. The other ducks soon joined in, and their instincts took over. Raised in tiny cages, they didn't know they loved water! Now they do, and they are forever changed.

This parable touches on a similar theme of resisting change—even if the change is toward a more wonderful life and regaining who we truly are.

Jesus' critics continually struggled with His teachings. His words were wonderful, yet a bit too new and edgy. Like the ducks, they resisted. All they knew was a restrictive cage of spiritual rules. In the proceeding verses to our parable (Luke 20:1–8) they, in essence, ask Jesus, "Who or what gives You the right to think You can change things up?" This was the context for this parable.

The story cleverly shows just who Jesus was, although they may have missed it. We simply cannot miss it. The beloved son of the vineyard owner represents Jesus. Jesus was and is the Son of God!

When Jesus was baptized, God couldn't help Himself and He called out for all to hear, "This is my Beloved Son, with whom I am well pleased" (Matt. 3:17). God acted like a proud father at a son's ballgame yelling out, "That's my boy!" At the transfiguration, God again spoke out, "This is my Beloved Son, with whom I am well pleased, listen to Him" (Matt. 17:5). And here, in the parable, Jesus speaks of a beloved son. Clearly, a reference to Himself.

Jesus was also making it clear He knew of their wishes to get rid of Him. It was as if Jesus were asking, "Are you really going to continue to resist My message and to plot My death?" Perhaps we too will be challenged by this parable and we must decide—what will we do with Jesus? Will we resist Him? Or will we allow Jesus to profoundly change our hearts?

Historical Context. Jesus used two themes in his parable that first-century Hebrews knew well. His story had a vineyard, and Israel was often referred to as a vine.

Let me sing for my beloved my love-song concerning his vineyard: My beloved had a vineyard on a very fertile hill (Isaiah 5:1 ESV).

Restore us, O God of hosts; let your face shine, that we may be saved. You brought a vine out of Egypt; you drove out the nations and planted it (Psalm 80:7–8 ESV).

Some ancient Jewish coins, as well as the first coin issued after Israel's independence in 1949, depicted a vine leaf with a cluster of grapes. It's a national symbol. It is a reference that would have stirred a positive emotion in their hearts. They would have placed themselves into the story as either the vineyard or caretakers.[1]

Jesus also used the idea of an absentee landowner. At the time of Christ, Palestine was a troubled, hard-to-endure place under Roman rule. Some Hebrew landowners departed for a safer way of life in foreign lands. Ancient writings describe agreements made between landowners and tenants. Tensions and conflicts are described, down to arguments over who should get the twigs left after pruning! Payment to the owner was often a percentage of the crop. So, the subject used in this parable of an absentee landowner would have been quite familiar to them.[2,3]

A landowner sending servants to fetch payment and to check on the condition of their prized land would have been expected. It is easy to imagine that it didn't always go well. The landowner might be disappointed if their land was being poorly cared for. The treatment given to the owner's servants and son, however, would have been viewed as nothing short of appalling.

Most theologians interpret this parable as an allegory with the landowner representing God, the servants representing prophets, the vineyard as His chosen people, the beloved son as Jesus, and the tenants as the religious leaders. The parable is thought to show God's patience, sending prophet after prophet, and eventually sending His own Son. It also shows God's love and care for His vineyard. And it prophetically points to the rejection and death of Jesus Himself.

We do have quite an appalling track record and history of mistreating our prophets. In the days of Elijah, many prophets were murdered. In the time of Joash, the people stoned Zechariah. Isaiah was sawed in two, according to tradition. The author of Hebrews sums it up (Heb. 11:35-38), describing prophets being tortured, mocked, imprisoned, afflicted, living destitute lives, or killed. That is not a great track record. In His parable, Jesus seems to invoke memories of this pitiful performance.

The Message. I believe parables are to be interpreted for the most part as metaphors and not allegories. In this case, however, the allegory symbolism seems hard to ignore. And seeing it as an allegory helps to answer their question on the authority of Jesus. Yet, it does not need to end there. What did Jesus intend this parable to teach you and me?

Something stands out to me. The owner, when pondering what to do after his third servant was severely beaten, considered sending his own son. *Perhaps they will respect him,* he thought. The word used here (*entrepo*) means to regard highly or to revere. The tenants clearly did not respect the servants, but maybe they will my son, the owner wondered.

We all want a little respect. It hurts when our ideas are ignored or when we feel unnoticed. But have you ever considered that God also desires respect? Our lives either show that we respect God or that we reject Him. When explaining the parable, Jesus invokes a reference to Psalm 118.

The stone the builders rejected has become the cornerstone (Psalm 118:22).

Jesus continues, "Everyone who falls on that stone will be broken to pieces; anyone on whom the stone falls will be crushed." Some of the message for us today is that we should respect what God desires to do in our hearts instead of pushing Him away. Pushing God away does not mean He goes away. He is always by our side.

God has wonderful work He wants to do in our hearts. We push back. We ignore Him or even rebel against Him. Yet, our emotional baggage, our wounds, and our untamed ego do not go away either. We just keep tripping over them, again and again. We must remember that all negative behavior stems from unprocessed pain. God wants us to gently process those hurts.

The first step toward change is awareness. The second step is acceptance. —Nathaniel Branden

God patiently and continually sends us invitations for healing. In Jesus' story, the tenants brutally beat each messenger and even killed his son. Jesus intensified their actions so we would not miss it.[4] Jesus wanted us to turn our heads in disgust, for their behavior was heinous and cruel.

Yet, the punch of the parable depends on just who you are in this story. Who am I? Well, let me break it to you. We are not the landowner (God), his beloved son (Jesus), or the servants (prophets), so it leaves us as either grapes or the tenants—you know, the same guys that caused us to look away? Yep, that's us!

We too very often reject Jesus! And like those caged ducks, we keep our heart in a cramped cage when it's dying to get out and grow. We think we enjoy overreacting, lashing out, judging, and desperately trying to be in control. Jesus wants us out of that cage! Jesus desires to unleash the love trapped inside our hearts. We often keep it caged up out of fear.

Jesus desires to restore us into caring and compassionate people—people who reflect who He is.

Instead, we choose to live out a lesser version of ourselves. We are very much like the ducks not knowing that we love water.

Let's remember who we are. Let's swim in the water of God's love.

Entering the Story

I don't understand Jesus sometimes. Once, He told me I need to be born again! Can you imagine? I am still trying to figure that one out.

I know Jesus is special. He is just so different. Many of my fellow Pharisees are writing Him off as another rebel zealot. To me, Jesus is more of a spiritual zealot. He wants to free us all right, just not so much from Rome but from ourselves.

As Pharisees, we meticulously adhere to God's laws. In Joshua, it says, "Keep the Law always on your lips; meditate on it day and night, so that you may be careful to do everything written in it. Then you will be prosperous and successful." This is what our God requires. We try our best to live this out.

I personally love Jesus' teachings. His words are life-giving. His understanding of scripture is profound. Yet, the last couple of days have been a little hard to handle, even for me. He rode into Jerusalem like a king. Enormous and adoring crowds shouted, "Blessed is the King who comes in the name of the Lord." Who do you think you are, Jesus?

Then, Jesus drove out merchants and money changers from the temple. He proclaimed, "You have made My house a den of robbers!" It was almost as if He were claiming the temple was His!

So, we asked Jesus, "What gives?" He told us a story.

He spoke of an owner of a vineyard who left for a foreign land. He placed tenants in charge. When the owner sent servants for the agreed share of the harvest, the tenants beat them and sent them back empty-handed. The owner finally sent his son, in hopes they would honor him, yet they killed him!

The tenants were so cruel! Many in the crowd shouted, "No way!" I thought to myself, *If I had been a tenant, I would never kill the owner's beloved son!*

Jesus said, "Then what is the meaning of Psalms: "The stone the builders rejected has become the capstone." Jesus is not inferring what I think He is, is He? Is Jesus saying that HE is the Son of God? John the Baptist claimed Jesus is the Chosen One, the Messiah, from God. Is Jesus now claiming this for Himself? If my fellow Pharisees were not infuriated already, they will be now!

Could this be true? As I wrestle with these thoughts, suddenly,

I am seeing Jesus as who He is—as God's One and Only Son. I feel an amazing calm and clarity come over me. I feel a peace that I have never felt before. It's as if God is washing me clean. I feel such love. All the scriptures I have spent my life memorizing, suddenly do not feel like rules to obey anymore but as a love letter.

I must tell the others. I must convince them before they do something harsh. Yet maybe I simply need to let Jesus do what He came to do. I'll let Jesus change my heart. I sense the need to simply enjoy His love.

I feel so alive and free. Suddenly, I feel...born again.

Living the Story

This is a challenging parable. Don't feel bad if it doesn't touch your heart right away. It will if you spend time with it. Ask God for the grace to hear His love through the parable.

- Have you ever marveled at a beautiful vineyard? What is your favorite wine? Think of the beautiful landscapes and the wonderful flavors, as you spend time with this parable.

- Be honest with yourself. How do you reject Jesus? How can you better honor and respect God in your life? What have you resisted turning over to God?

- Try re-writing the parable using something special to you that you enjoy taking care of. Imagine God

Point of the Parable:

Stop resisting God's invitation for life and growth.

We often ignore God. All the while, he sends us invite after invite for rest and renewal.

Jesus said, "Don't reject My Son, for He is your cornerstone."

Allowing Jesus into every area of your life is how to discover who you truly are.

asking you for His fair share. Do you resist? Journal your thoughts and emotions.

- For a duck, time in the water is refreshing and relaxing. It's harder for them to walk on land. What are ways you try to control situations, protect your ego, and as a result, exhaust yourself? Ask God to show you how you can simply let go and float on the water of His love.[5]

A Blessing for You,
as You Accept God's Invitation

May you know God will never give up on you. He sends invite after invite for you to grow closer and to experience more of Him. May you know and feel that you are God's beloved. God delights in you. God shouts over you, "That's My son! That's My daughter!"

May you ask God to show you when and how you push Him away or ignore His loving call. May God's voice be recognizable and His ways clear.

May you completely trust God. He will be loving and gentle with your heart. God has your best in mind. May you say yes to His love.

22

One Thing

For where your treasure is, there your heart will be also (Matt. 6:21).

The kingdom of heaven is like treasure hidden in a field. When a man found it, he hid it again, and then in his joy went and sold all he had and bought that field.

Again, the kingdom of heaven is like a merchant looking for fine pearls. When he found one of great value, he went away and sold everything he had and bought it (Matt. 13:44–46).

Listening to the Story

If you could have one thing and only one thing, what would it be?

For the characters in these fascinating little stories, their respective one thing was hidden treasure and a pearl. What is your one thing? Is it your family, a degree, or a certain position? Perhaps it is early retirement. Or perhaps your one thing is a deep friendship with God.

Maybe life's quest is to wrestle with this very question. Let me warn you, these two little parables may get you thinking and rock your world. I hope you find wrestling with these little parables from Matthew to be the perfect conclusion to our journey through Luke's parables.

In the movie *City Slickers,* Mitch (played by Billy Crystal) was on a quest to get back his smile and zest for life. Mitch hoped a two-week, cattle-herding, adventure in the wild west would do it. A hard-as-nails, untamed, mustang-of-a-man, trail boss named Curly let him know that all he needed to do was find his "one thing."

The challenge for Mitch was to find his one purpose in life. Through a difficult and near-death experience of a river crossing, Mitch realized his one thing was his family.

I agree with Curly. Finding our one thing is how we too can live a rich and meaningful life.

Jesus often uses odd characters and story lines for His parables. Let's take a look.

A Man in a Field. Jesus compared the kingdom of God to a treasure hidden in a field. A man finds it, hides it again, sells everything to buy the field, and the treasure is his! To me, this seems a tad odd and even a little devious. If the man was brimming with integrity, wouldn't he have told the landowner of his rightful treasure?

We learned from the "Love over Fear" parable (Luke 19:11–27) that it was common for people to bury money to protect it. Rabbis commonly taught such tactics (Baba Metzia 42a).[1] Josephus tells of wealth hidden by the Jews that the Romans tried to find.[2]

Buried treasure always has an original owner and the man who lucked upon it could have tried to find that owner. Instead, he devised a scheme, in hopes that the landowner was unaware of the treasure so he could gain it for himself. His devious scheme worked.

A Merchant. Jesus then compared the kingdom of God not to a pearl, but to a merchant in search of one. A life dedicated to treasure hunting is wonderfully odd. Merchants (*emporos*) in that day were not respected. Sirach 26:29 states, "A merchant can hardly keep from wrongdoing, nor is a tradesman innocent of sin" (NRSV). The term carried the connotation of a salesman, perhaps one who markets items most people do not need at a cost very few could afford.

A merchant sold Joseph into slavery (Gen. 37:28), and when Jesus got upset in the temple, He cried out, "Stop making my Father's house a marketplace!" (John 2:16, *emporiou*).[3]

Maybe for us today, it's how we might view a pawn shop dealer, although there is nothing inherently wrong with owning a pawn shop! Or perhaps how we view an adventurous modern treasure hunter who searches the oceans for sunken ships that carried large bounties of gold. Let's admit it; these aren't your standard professions we think about for our kids. Yet, Jesus delightfully uses these odd characters.

These two individuals certainly provide some exciting mystery. Is Jesus encouraging being devious or dedicating our life to treasure hunting? I don't think so. Yet, that's part of the punch of these juicy little parables. You see, if these devious characters know a treasure when they find one, if they are willing to sacrifice everything for it, how about us? As usual, Jesus is using extremes to make a point.

Finally, let's take a look at the treasure itself.

A Pearl. In the ancient world, pearls were extremely valuable. In fact, pearls were regarded as the most valuable objects in existence. As a result, a pearl was a symbol of supreme worth.[4] Perhaps the best way to see how valuable pearls were in the ancient world is through another story from antiquity.

Pliny the Elder (who died in 79 A.D.) penned the book, *Natural History.* It was a colossal work describing all the knowledge at that time contained in natural history and science. He described a banquet served by Cleopatra VII for her Roman lover, Marc Anthony. In a rather brash display of her wealth and power, Cleopatra makes a bet with Marc Antony that she could spend 10 million sesterces (sounds like a lot!) on one single meal.

She ordered the second course to be served. In accordance with previous instructions, the servants placed in front of her a single vessel containing only vinegar. She took one of her pearl earrings off and dropped it in the vinegar. When it wasted away, she swallowed it.

And the pearl was not just any pearl. Pliny called it, "The largest in the whole of history, a remarkable and truly unique work of nature," worth 10 million sesterces.

I think I would have liked this gal, Cleopatra. She had some spunk!

This fascinating story, true or not, shows the intrigue and love of pearls at the time of Christ. Yet Jesus, a poor man from a rural village, likely never knew how a pearl felt swirling around in His palm. Doesn't that touch your heart? Jesus, the master Storyteller, uses a pearl to represent an invaluable treasure and the loveliest of all possessions.

The Message. The metaphor of the treasure-finding field worker and treasure-hunting merchant should cause us to slow down and take stock of our own lives. And unlike Mitch, we don't need to be on a cattle drive to do so (although it might not hurt).

These parables alone should cause you to do some reflecting. What is your highest priority in life? Are you willing to sacrifice everything else to get it? What is of ultimate value for you?[5]

Those who know where the treasure lies, joyfully abandon everything else to secure it. –D.A. Carson

That is not all. These parables teach us a few other things. For one, we should never be ashamed of being on a spiritual quest. The merchant was on a lifelong pursuit. We are all on a quest for answers to our questions. Going to God with our questions only strengthens our intimacy. Faith can take a huge hit when trouble comes if we have never wrestled with the deep questions of life.

These parables also teach that life should be an adventure. That is worth repeating. Life with Christ should be a wonderful adventure! How dare we make it boring or dutiful! Jesus told these little adventure stories to illustrate that life is to be enjoyed.

But let's get back to the main point of the parable. If you could have one thing and only one thing, what would it be? This is worthwhile to ponder. It's okay to be honest even if your answer is something different than God. You may have a few treasures. It's important to be sincere with God. If your goal is to make God Himself your treasure, please realize that it will take time. It will take time with Him! It will take intentional time basking in His love for you.

What may help us on our quest is to realize that we are God's "one thing." You read that right! On more than one occasion, God calls us, "The apple of his eye" (Psalm 17:8, Zech. 2:8). We are God's ultimate treasure! We are God's one thing!

So, is the parable a metaphor for God finding His treasure in us, or for us finding our treasure in Him? Maybe, just maybe, it is both. Intriguing, isn't it?

You are worth everything to Jesus.

You are God's one thing! What is yours?

Entering the Story

"You and your stories," I said to Jesus. "Jesus, you tell so many of them! Sometimes they make my head spin," I said with a chuckle. I could be honest with Jesus. He grinned with delight. He knew I loved His stories. He could see my face beam in excitement as He told them.

Today would be such a day. Jesus spoke of a field worker who finds a treasure. Now that is speaking my language. I work the fields. I work for Jewish landowners at planting and harvest time, or whenever they need hired help.

I am not originally from Palestine. I am not even a Jew. Nor am I a Roman. I brought my family here in search of work. Romans rule this land. They are the top of society. Yet, the Jews are a proud people; they love to tell me of their great history as God's chosen ones and how someday they will again get their land back.

So, that pretty much puts me at the bottom of society here, but I don't really mind. I earn enough to feed my family and for that I am grateful.

I love Jesus. We have become dear friends. When I am not working, I go listen to His stories. His story today of a field worker especially spoke to me. I think I knew its message.

It's message is to have Jesus as my treasure! And for me, He is! And my precious family is also my treasure! Being content in who I am, being honest, and working with integrity are also treasures. I do not have to go digging for them. I have no need to set sail to a foreign land in search of anything. I have all the treasure I need. At least these were the thoughts that were swirling around in my head as I listened.

As Jesus was telling these stories, I imagined wearing a band of jewels around my neck. Funny, I know! On my band was a jewel of contentment, jewels of family, love, and gratitude. These are my jewels. Yet, the center and largest gem is my friend, Jesus. He is my favorite. I grinned as I imagined my necklace.

Jesus could see my delight and asked me if I understood the parable of the hidden treasure. I told him what I was thinking, and I said, "Jesus, I found my treasure, and it's You!" He giggled in delight and said He had one last parable to tell me.

Heaven is like the master of a household who brings out of his treasure what is new and what is old (Matt. 13:52 NRSV).

Jesus smiled, leaned into my ear, and whispered so only I could hear. I will never forget his tender words.

"You are God's treasure. God delights in you!"

"I love you more than you'll ever know."

Living the Story

There is an interesting contrast between our two parables. The field worker happens on his treasure by chance, almost as though the treasure found him. In contrast, the merchant was on a lifelong quest to find his. This shows a beautiful juxtaposition of truths. We may be on a quest to find God, but God is also on a quest to find us!

- Spend time remembering the many times God has lovingly pursued you. How has He tangibly done that in your life? Thank God for continually seeking you out.

- Next, recall times you earnestly sought God for His love and direction, and He revealed Himself to you. How was your life changed?

I believe much of our spiritual growth is learning to surrender to whatever we are holding too tightly. As we loosen our grip on things that feel important, and instead, cling to God as our one thing, our lives will become richly more meaningful.

- What is of ultimate importance in your life, right now? Are you happy with that? What do you want your pearl to be? Journal how you are going to find it.

Point of the Parable:

You are God's most important thing. What's yours?

If you could only have one thing, what would it be?

Jesus said, "Find your perfect pearl like the treasure-hunter found his."

We are all on a journey to find our one thing. God found his, it's you!

• What is God asking you to loosen your grip on or to even let go of?

A Blessing for You, the Treasure-Seeker

And now, may your life become a parable of adventure as you discover your one thing buried deep and secure in the heart of God. May you find the thing that no one can ever take from you.

May God, who lovingly created you as His treasure, take away the load of what worries you today. May He meet you exactly where you are, even if you are in the depths of despair with little hope in sight.

May you know and feel like the rarest of all treasures to God—because that is who you are!

May you feel safe in the arms of your Savior and friend. May you know that God delights in you, with no expectation for you to change.

May you delight in the fact that you are God's one thing.

Appendix

Interpreting the Parables

The best way to interpret the parables is to be willing to hear them anew. A good storyteller creates a new world for you to enter. The key is to enter that world without preconceived ideas.

Parables are vivid stories to convince us to change our attitude or behavior. They allow us to see God's character in a new way. They help us know and love God more deeply. Here are a few helpful tools to help us make a sound interpretation, as adapted from Synodgrass.[1]

- If the parable is told by more than one gospel writer, examine each one and compare the possible different perspectives from each gospel writer.

- Listen to the parable through the ears of the original first century hearers. They are short stories, spoken *from* a Hebrew *to* fellow Hebrews. Whatever we can do to help us understand the culture and context is important. Pay attention to the question or challenge given to Jesus setting up why He told it.

- Remember the parable was intended to illustrate or enhance a truth He may have just told. Put the parable in the context of the truth Jesus told directly before or after the parable. Any interpretation should also fit Jesus' greater teachings.

- Twenty-two of the parables start with a question, such as, "Who of you...." Even when an explicit question is not present, finding the implicit question the parable was intended to answer is helpful.

- Interpret what is *given*, not what is *excluded* from the story. Jesus' stories are noticeably short and leave out many details. This is by design. Do not try and give meaning to why something was excluded.

- Pay attention to the ending of the story. Often the ending packs a punch! Sometimes, the ending is meant to shock or surprise. Most often, what comes at the ending is a clue to its intent and is often the most important part of the story. So, focus on it.

The initial goal is to arrive at what the story would have meant to its original, first century audience. This helps us arrive at the message for us as well.

Interpreting the parables in this way is where to begin. Yet, I believe God invites you to go deeper still! He desires to speak to you in a more intimate way with a message that pierces your heart and draws you closer to His infinite love. The way to this is through imaginative prayer, which is described in "Experiencing the Parables."

Experiencing the Parables

Imaginative prayer is the suggested path for getting to a richer, more personal message. It's not so much interpreting the parable as it is letting the parable interpret you! This allows for Jesus to personally speak to you.

The following suggestions will help you engage with the parables as never before. They will help you *experience* the parables, not simply *read* them.

- Prayerfully ask God to quiet your heart and to open your imagination to Him.

- Read the passage and notice if there was a question or challenge brought to Jesus which initiated Him telling the parable. Now, imagine yourself having that same question. Notice the common everyday objects from nature or people that Jesus used. Notice the simple, main elements and characters of the story.

- Read the parable again and now imagine yourself in the setting of Jesus' telling the parable. Are you inside or outside? What season is it? What's the temperature? Try and imagine the setting with as much detail as you can. Compose the scene in your mind. Be one of His original hearers. Have fun with this!

- Now, close your eyes and let the story unfold in your mind. Imagine Jesus telling it just to you. How does the story impact your feelings? Are you angry, sad, or surprised? Pay attention to those feelings and your reaction. What character are you drawn to within the parable? Be honest, even if the character is the seemingly less attractive one. Journaling will greatly help. Allow the words to flow.

- Now, it gets good. Imagine yourself having a conversation with Jesus after He tells the story. As Nathan told David, "You are the man," what does Jesus say to you? What is the reason Jesus wanted you to hear and experience this story? Respond back to Jesus. Tell Jesus your feelings. Then allow Him to respond. Journal your experience. Do not force this, but if it comes, allow God to speak wonderful things to you. You will only hear words of love if it is truly from God.

You may also try to re-craft the parable into a similar yet meaningful story. Have your story convey the same message yet write it as a meaningful metaphor from your life. Make it simple, inspiring, with a similar ending punch.

It simply does not make sense that the parables were only to be heard as a story once in history. God wants you to share in the excitement as well!

Notes

Chapter 1: The Power of a Story

1. Renken, Elena., "How Stories Connect and Persuade us: Unleashing the Brain Power of Narrative," npr.org, April 11, 2020.
2. Donahue, John R., SJ. *The Gospel in Parable*. Minneapolis, MN: Fortress Press, 1988, 18–19. (It's great to have a genuine example from Scripture of the power of a parable and how it can change behavior. Thanks David.)
3. Snodgrass, Klyne R. *Stories with Intent: A Comprehensive Guide to the Parables of Jesus*. Grand Rapids, MI: William B. Eerdman's Publishing Company, 2008, 1. (Snodgrass crafted a massive work, intended for scholars, providing great background and historical information for each parable. I have gleaned from his work.)
4. Ibid., 22.
5. Barclay, William. *The Parables of Jesus*. Louisville, KY: Westminster John Knox Press, 1970, 12. (Barclay's strength is his understanding of 1st-century culture, which is a love of mine as well.)
6. Snodgrass, 7.
7. Bolz-Weber, Nadia, "Sermon on the Worst Parable Ever," *Sojourners*. October 23, 2011. (How could I not use this brilliant and funny summary of the parables from Nadia. I have altered her original words a little. Nadia always tells it like it is, and I often glean inspiration from this "Accidental Saint.")
8. Dodd, C.H., *The Parables of the Kingdom*. NY: Charles Scribner's Sons, 1961, 5. (Dodd's definition has served us well for 60 years. I've altered it somewhat but he nicely hit on the important aspects; parables are for the most part metaphors and not allegories, Jesus' use of everyday events, and the parables odd yet special appeal. It's like an intriguing yet scary movie; hard to watch but you can't look away. His definition also brings out that we should use our imagination and that they contain wonderful applications. Well done, Dodd!)
9. Snodgrass, 2.
10. Levine, Amy-Jill. *Short Stories by Jesus: The Enigmatic Parables of a Controversial Rabbi*. San Francisco: HarperOne, 2014, 94. (Levine wonderfully brings out a much-needed Jewish understanding to the parables.)

11. Dodd, 12.
12. Barclay, 13.
13. Donahue, 10.
14. Martin, James SJ. *Jesus: A Pilgrimage.* San Francisco: HarperOne, 2014, 205. (Martin is always a joy to read and his thought that Jesus' life was like a parable caused, for me, a "Darn, why didn't I think of that?" moment.)
15. Martin, 206.
16. Snodgrass, 23.

Chapter 2: In with the New

1. Barclay, William. *The Gospel of Luke.* Philadelphia: The Westminster Press, 1975, 66.
2. Kennedy, AL. "A Point of View: Why embracing change is the key to happiness." BBC News, December 8, 2013, https://www.bbc.com/news/magazine-23986212 .
3. Barclay, 67.

Chapter 3: Eyes to See

1. Dekker, Rebecca, PhD, RN, "The Evidence on: Erythromycin Eye Ointment for Newborns", *Evidenced Based Birth,* November 12, 2012. (For anything medical, I seek the advice of a doctor.)
2. Schaller, U. C., & Klauss, V., "Is Credé's Prophylaxis for Ophthalmia Neonatorum Still Valid?", *World Health Organization,* 2001, 262–263.
3. Tristram, H.B., D.D., Eastern Customs in Bible Lands, London: Hodder and Stoughton, 1894, 12. (This is one of my favorite sources of 1st-century Palestinian culture. The book is hard to find. My copy is very used. It came from a library in Paris (Ontario, that is. France would have been more impressive.) The pages resemble parchment and some of them were never separated properly by the publishing house. Tristram traveled extensively, was a true historian and scientist (an Ornithologist). He wrote extensively. He was old-school British. Do I love his work? Indeed.)
4. Barclay, William, *The Gospel of Luke,* Philadelphia: The Westminster Press, 1975, 81.
5. Rohr, Fr. Richard, OFM, "The Dualistic Mind", *Center for Action and Contemplation,* January 29, 2017. (Thank you, Father Rohr, for teaching me about dualism.)

Chapter 4: Digging Deep

1. Barclay, William, *The Parables of Jesus,* Louisville, KY: Westminster John Knox Press, 1970, 217. (I have had the privilege of traveling extensively throughout the Middle East and seeing Wadis for myself and the damage they can cause after a heavy rain. Growing up in Arizona helped as well. As a Geological Engineer, I appreciate the value of a good foundation. Building projects that do not consider geology simple do not last. If you build in a flood plain, an area prone to earthquakes or landslides—a proper foundation is critical.)
2. Ibid., 218. (Don't you love it that Jesus worked with his hands and with wood? I sure do. Jesus understands the grain of wood and the soul within each of us!)
3. Snodgrass, Klyne R., *Stories with Intent: A Comprehensive Guide to the Parables of Jesus,* Grand Rapids, MI: William B. Eerdman's Publishing Company, 2008, 333.
4. Boice, James Montgomery, *The Parables of Jesus,* Chicago: Moody Publishers, 1983, 141–142.
5. Snodgrass, 337.

Chapter 5: Better than Bad

1. Barclay, William, *The Gospel of Luke,* Philadelphia: The Westminster Press, 1975, 94.
2. Wailes, Stephen L, *Medieval Allegories of Jesus' Parables,* University of California Press, 1987, 173–177.
3. Snodgrass, Klyne R., *Stories with Intent: A Comprehensive Guide to the Parables of Jesus,* Grand Rapids, MI: William B. Eerdman's Publishing Company, 2008, 82.
4. Barclay, 94.

Chapter 6: Sower and Soil

1. Wright, Tom, "The Kingdom New Testament: A Contemporary Translation", HarperOne, 2011, 25.
2. Snodgrass, Klyne R., *Stories with Intent: A Comprehensive Guide to the Parables of Jesus,* Grand Rapids, MI: William B. Eerdman's Publishing Company, 2008, 155.
3. Ibid., 155.
4. Boice, James Montgomery, *The Parables of Jesus,* Chicago: Moody Publishers, 1983, 16–20.

5. Bolz-Weber, Nadia, July 2010 sermon and blog posting. (This is inspired from Nadia, from a sermon of hers. Nadia, once again, says it like it is in her wonderfully crass way.)

6. Martin, James, SJ, *Jesus: A Pilgrimage,* HarperOne, 2014, 199. (The parables may touch you in this way; not so much describing different individuals, but different parts of you! If they do, stay with it, and prayerfully ponder the parts of you that need changing.)

Chapter 7: Good Bad Guy

1. McClaren, Brian D., *A New Kind of Christian: A Tale of Two Friends on a Spiritual Journey,* Jossey-Bass, 2001.

2. Levine, Amy-Jill, *Short Stories by Jesus: The enigmatic Parables of a Controversial Rabbi,* San Francisco: HarperOne, 2014, 84–86. (Thinking we need to somehow earn God's approval can easily creep into our lives and thoughts. It's a part of being human. It can be hard to accept undeserved love, but that is what God gives.)

3. Barclay, William, *The Gospel of Luke,* Philadelphia: The Westminster Press, 1975, 140.

4. Levine, 106.

5. Barclay, William, *The Parables of Jesus,* Louisville, KY: Westminster John Knox Press, 1970, 79. (Even today, the road is somewhat isolated and remote, and you can get a sense as to why Jesus chose this road for his parable.)

6. Snodgrass, Klyne R., *Stories with Intent: A Comprehensive Guide to the Parables of Jesus,* Grand Rapids, MI: William B. Eerdman's Publishing Company, 2008, 345.

Chapter 8: Friend in Need

1. Snodgrass, Klyne R., *Stories with Intent: A Comprehensive Guide to the Parables of Jesus,* Grand Rapids, MI: William B. Eerdmans Publishing, 2008, 441.

2. Barclay, William, *The Parables of Jesus,* Westminster John Knox Press, 1970, 113.

3. Snodgrass, 448.

Chapter 9: Hitting It Big

1. Snodgrass, Klyne R., *Stories with Intent: A Comprehensive Guide to*

the Parables of Jesus, Grand Rapids, MI: William B. Eerdman's Publishing Company, 2008, 400.

2. Ibid., 394.

3. Barclay, William, *The Gospel of Luke,* Philadelphia: The Westminster Press, 1975, 164. (A nice illustration from Barclay. We all can be like Edith. Our natural tendency is to look out for ourselves. Once we are ok, we feel more at ease to consider others' needs. God calls us to consider others before ourselves—that takes grace.)

4. Boice, James Montgomery, *The Parables of Jesus,* Chicago: Moody Publishers, 1983, 123.

5. Bolz-Weber, Nadia, "Sermon on Losing Your Life and How Jesus Isn't Your Magical Puppy", Sojourners, March 15, 2012. (Nadia gives a poignant and fitting illustration.)

Chapter 10: Being Ready

1. Blomberg, Craig L., *Interpreting the Parables,* Downers Grove, IL: InterVarsity Press, 1990, 191. (Christian groups can be so hard on themselves, especially when they feel the need for policing "bad behavior" within their constituents. Yet, those in authority who abuse the vulnerable are at times sadly and pitifully overlooked.)

2. Barclay, William, *The Gospel of Luke,* Philadelphia: Westminster Press, 1975, 168.

Chapter 11: Where's the Fruit

1. Gaebelein, Frank E., *The Expositor's Bible Commentary*, Volume 8, Grand Rapids, MI: Regency Reference Library, 1984, 970.

2. Barclay, William, *The Gospel of Luke,* Philadelphia: Westminster Press, 1975, 172–173.

3. Ibid., 173–174.

4. Richardson, James Rev., "Fig Tress in the Vineyard?", *Church of the Incarnation,* February 28, 2016.

5. Bolz-Weber, Nadia, "One More Year for Figs and Manure", *House for All Sinners and Saints,* March 4, 2013.

Chapter 12: Little into a Lot

1. Snodgrass, Klyne R., *Stories with Intent: A Comprehensive Guide to the Parable of Jesus,* Grand Rapids, MI: William B. Eerdmans Publishing Company, 2008, 220. (It really does not matter if there are

seeds smaller than the mustard seed. At the time of Jesus, the mustard seed was thought to be the smallest and so it was a perfect metaphor for Jesus to use.)

2. Levine, Amy-Jill, *Short Stories by Jesus: The Enigmatic Parable of a Controversial Rabbi,* San Francisco: Harper One, 1989, 121. (Those who enjoy using sourdough starter or brewing kombucha (which involves maintaining a living scoby) can perhaps appreciate this parable even more. I made Kombucha for around six months. Maintaining the living, growing scoby was super weird but fun until it wasn't!)

3. Ibid., 133.

4. Snodgrass, 220.

5. Meyers, Carol, *Households and Holiness: The Religious Culture of Israelite Women,* Minneapolis: Fortress, 2005.

Chapter 13: Time for a Feast

1. Barclay, William, *The Parables of Jesus,* Louisville, KY: Westminster John Knox Press, 1970, 151.

2. Gaebelein, Frank E., *The Expositor's Bible Commentary,* Volume 8, Grand Rapids, MI: Regency Reference Library, 1984, 978.

3. Tristram, H.B., D.D., *Eastern Customs in Bible Lands,* London: Hodder and Stoughton, 1894, 83.

4. Donahue, John R. S.J., *The Gospel in Parable,* Fortress Press, 1988, 141.

5. Keating, Thomas, *The Kingdom of God is Like...,* New York: Crossroad Publishing, 1993, 68.

Chapter 14: It'll Cost You

1. Barclay, William, *The Gospel of Luke,* Philadelphia: The Westminster Press, 1975, 197.

2. Barclay, William, *The Parables of Jesus,* Louisville, KY: Westminster John Knox Press, 1970, 204.

3. Snodgrass, Klyne R., *Stories with Intent: A Comprehensive Guide to the Parable of Jesus,* Grand Rapids, MI: William B. Eerdmans Publishing Company, 2008, 380–383.

4. Barclay, 207.

5. Ibid., 207.

Chapter 15: Lost and Found

1. Barclay, William, *The Parables of Jesus,* Louisville, KY: Westminster John Knox Press, 1970, 177.
2. Ibid., 179
3. Levine, Amy-Jill, *Short Stories by Jesus: The enigmatic Parables of a Controversial Rabbi,* San Francisco: HarperOne, 2014, 43. (Levine does such a good job with this parable, pointing out the cultural undercurrents that we may otherwise miss.)
4. Barclay, 180.
5. Tristram, H.B., D.D., *Eastern Customs in Bible Lands,* London: Hodder and Stoughton, 1894, 76–77.
6. Levine, 51.
7. Bolz-Weber, Nadia, "The Parable of the Prodigal Father", patheos.com, March 11, 2013. (If you are like me, you can probably see yourself at times as the younger brother and other times as the older. And some parts of yourself may fall into a silly squandering category and in other parts, you may proudly have it all together. Extremes at either end may not be healthy. Ponder what those might be for you.)

Chapter 16: Being Shrewd

1. Boice, James Montgomery, *The Parables of Jesus,* Chicago: Moody Publishers, 1983, 132.
2. Snodgrass, Klyne R., *Stories with Intent: A Comprehensive Guide to the Parables of Jesus,* Grand Rapids, MI: William B. Eerdman's Publishing Company, 2008, 406.
3. Ibid., 406
4. Barclay, William, *The Parables of Jesus,* Louisville, KY: Westminster John Knox Press, 1970, 148–149.
5. Ibid., 148–149.
6. Ibid., 148–149.

Chapter 17: Poor Rich Man

1. Levine, Amy-Jill, *Short Stories by Jesus: The Enigmatic Parables of a Controversial Rabbi,* San Francisco: HarperOne, 2014, 271.
2. Snodgrass, Klyne R., *Stories with Intent: A Comprehensive Guide to the Parables of Jesus,* Grand Rapids, MI: William B. Eerdman's

Publishing Company, 2008, 406. (For me this is hard to imagine. People boiling snails for days in large, lead vats to create purple dye. I picture slaves working this smelly, nasty, never-ending job—all so royalty and the rich can adorn themselves with this color, flaunting their wealth. In Egypt, I was forever changed when I witnessed peasants working open smelters, melting old batteries. The endeavor to recycle was to be commended, but the working conditions were atrocious.)

3. Levine, 271–273.
4. Levine, 274.
5. Boice, James Montgomery, *The Parables of Jesus,* Chicago: Moody Publishers, 1983, 239. (Boice inspired my title for this parable.)
6. Barclay, William, *The Parables of Jesus,* Louisville, KY: Westminster John Knox Press, 1970, 97.
7. Bouquet, A.C., *Everyday Life in New Testament Times*, New York: Charles Scribner's Sons, 1953, 143.
8. Assisi Animal Health, "Why Do Dogs Lick their Wounds," assisianimalhealth.com, August 12, 2013.
9. Levine, 282.
10. Levine, 296.

Chapter 18: Relentless for Justice

1. Barclay, William, *The Parables of Jesus*, Louisville, KY: Westminster John Knox Press, 1970, 114–115.
2. Tristram, H. B., *Eastern Customs of Bible Lands*, New York: Thomas Whitaker, 1894, 228–229. (We do not know the date for this true story, but it's vivid detail and resemblance to our parable make it invaluable.)
3. Snodgrass, Klyne R., *Stories with Intent: A Comprehensive Guide to the Parables of Jesus*, Grand Rapids, MI: William B. Eerdman's Publishing Company, 2008, 458.
4. Levine, Amy-Jill, *Short Stories by Jesus: The Enigmatic Parables of a Controversial Rabbi*, San Francisco: HarperOne, 2014, 253–254.
5. Snodgrass, 453.
6. Hylen, Susan E., "Widows in the New Testament Period", The Bible and Interpretation, February 2019, bibleinterp.arizona.edu.
7. Ibid.
8. Bolz-Weber, Nadia, "A Standing Applause Sermon: The Persistent

God," Views from the Edge, Fourth Presbyterian Church, gordonc-stewart.com.

Chapter 19: Lord have Mercy

1. Gaebelein, Frank E., *The Expositor's Bible Commentary*, Volume 8, Grand Rapids, MI: Regency Reference Library, 1984, Volume 8, 1002.
2. Snodgrass, Klyne R., *Stories with Intent: A Comprehensive Guide to the Parables of Jesus*, Grand Rapids, MI: William B. Eerdman's Publishing Company, 2008, 467.
3. Barclay, William, *The Parables of Jesus*, Louisville, KY: Westminster John Knox Press, 1970, 100.
4. Levine, Amy-Jill, *Short Stories by Jesus: The Enigmatic Parables of a Controversial Rabbi*, San Francisco: HarperOne, 2014, 200–202.
5. Ibid., 187. (It's natural to view the Pharisees in an immediate negative light. Back in their day, they were highly respected. We must understand that when reading the parables.)
6. Barclay, William, *The Parables of Jesus*, Louisville, KY: Westminster John Knox Press, 1970, 101.
7. Ibid.
8. Snodgrass, 466.
9. Toumanova, Nina, Savin, Olga (did the translating from Russian), "The Way of the Pilgrim," Boston & London: Shambhala Publications, 1991. (This is a fun and heartwarming little read about a pilgrim's journey with the Jesus Prayer.)
10, Brown, Dr. Brene, "The Power of Vulnerability", Ted Talks. (Brown's work on vulnerability is first class.)

Chapter 20: Love Over Fear

1. Barclay, William, *The Parables of Jesus*, Louisville, KY: Westminster John Knox Press, 1970, 174.
2. Snodgrass, Klyne R., *Stories with Intent: A Comprehensive Guide to the Parables of Jesus*, Grand Rapids, MI: William B. Eerdman's Publishing Company, 2008, 521. (It is so helpful when authors bring out what Josephus had to say. Reading his large volume of work for yourself, although certainly worthwhile, would be difficult.)
3. Blomberg, Craig L., *Interpreting the Parables*, Downers Grove, IL: Intervarsity Press, 1990, 215.

4. Colier, Nancy LCSW, Rev., "Choosing Love not Fear", Psychology Today, February 22, 2018, psychologytoday.com.

Chapter 21: Resisting Change

1. Boice, James Montgomery, *The Parables of Jesus*, Chicago: Moody Publishing, 1983, 219.
2. Barclay, William, *The Parables of Jesus*, Louisville, KY: Westminster John Knox Press, 1970, 140.
3. Snodgrass, Klyne R., *Stories with Intent: A Comprehensive Guide to the Parables of Jesus*, Grand Rapids, MI: William B. Eerdman's Publishing Company, 2008, 284.
4. Jeremias, Joachim, *The Parables of Jesus*, New Jersey: Prentice-Hall, 2nd Edition, 1972, 76.
5. Benner, David G., *Surrender to Love: Discovering the Heart of Christian Spirituality*, Downers Grove, IL: Intervarsity Press, 2005.

Chapter 22: One Thing

1. Blomberg, Craig L. *Interpreting the Parables*. Downers Grove, IL, 1990, 215.
2. Snodgrass, Klyne R. *Stories with Intent: A Comprehensive Guide to the Parables of Jesus*. Grand Rapids, MI: William B. Eerdman's Publishing Company, 2008, 241.
3. Levine, Amy-Jill. *Short Stories by Jesus: The Enigmatic Parables of a Controversial Rabbi*. Participant Guide by Mario Mayo, Nashville, TN: Abingdon Press, 1988, 142–44.
4. Snodgrass, 250.
5. Levine 161.

Appendix

1. Snodgrass, Klyne R., *Stories with Intent: A Comprehensive Guide to the Parables of Jesus*, Grand Rapids, MI: William B. Eerdman's Publishing Company, 2008, 17–21.

About the Author

Samuel C. Hughes is a certified spiritual director and retired geological engineer. He is passionate in his pursuit of a deeply grounded, intimate personal life with God, which fuels his heart for everything. Samuel enjoys integrating sound biblical interpretation with contemplative practices. His goal is an awakened heart to love and a transformed life to share with others. (Spoiler alert—Samuel is the first to admit he has a long way to go on his journey!)

The parables have been a passion for Samuel for many years. He has crafted a unique approach to understanding Jesus' stories, which includes allowing one's imagination to bring the parables to life. Samuel developed a deep love for imaginative prayer by engaging in an eight-month journey through the "Ignatian Exercises in Everyday Life." The journey was life-changing.

Living and serving many years in various foreign cultures (Egypt, Kuwait, Pakistan, and Indonesia) has given Samuel a unique perspective and appreciation for diverse people. Samuel has an unquenchable curiosity for the first-century culture of Palestine, the unique palette Jesus entered and used to paint His wonderfully curious stories, the parables. His parables are intended to stir our hearts into a better understanding of His nature, ourselves, and His love-perspective for life—like only a story can.

Samuel has always loved an adventure and trying new things, whether running new high mountain trails, learning different woodworking skills, or enjoying unique ways to experience God's love. Samuel's primary passion is his family, being married to his best friend for 41 years and enjoying the best kids and grandkids a guy could ever have.

In short, his heartbeat is basking in God's infinite love and bringing others along for the ride.

I have never quit loving you and never will. Expect love, love, and more love (Jeremiah 31:3 The Message).

Wishes

New apartment
Back to work
Chance attending church
Financial freedom
Cleaning

Precautions

Chance's friends
Chance + school + grades
My health

CPSIA information can be obtained
at www.ICGtesting.com
Printed in the USA
LVHW051504121121
703156LV00009B/153